For Jennifer —

This is Mediterranean
Israel — a different
side of Israel than
most people think
about —

Neil & Anne
Folberg

A Love Story

in
Mediterranean
Israel

Memoir by Lin Arison

Photographs by Neil Folberg

Special thanks to the following people for their instrumental role in developing this book: Allen Hoffman, for his developmental editing and encouragement from the beginning; Neil Folberg, for his stunning photographs; Monika Stout of Tehabi Books, for her design, art direction, and art production; Betsy Holt of Tehabi Books, for her project editing; Avital Moses, for her ongoing assistance; and Tracey Corwin for her help, especially distribution.

ISBN 1-931688-00-1

The paper used in this publication meets the minimum requirements of the American National Standard for Information Sciences-Permanence of Paper for Printed Library Materials, ANSI Z39.48-1992.

First Edition
Printed through Dai Nippon Printing Co., Ltd. in Korea.
10 9 8 7 6 5 4 3 2 1

Illustrations
Denise Hilton-Campbell: 1, 15, 29, 37, 39, 45, 49, 50b, 55, 59, 69, 75, 83, 93, 95, 99, 103, 110, 113, 115, 123, 129, 133, 137, 138, 145, 150, 157, 159, 168

Photographs
©Barbara Burian Howe/CORBIS: 30-31
©CORBIS: 14-15, 18, 26-27, 40
©Galen Rowell/CORBIS: 28-29
©Jack Hillingsworth/CORBIS: 20
©Lee Snider; Lee Snider/CORBIS: 16-17
Lin Arison: 31
©Mike Zens/CORBIS: 126-127
©Morton Beebe, S.F./CORBIS: 22-23, 122-123
Neal Folberg Gallery: 2-3, 4-5, 6-7, 7, 8-9, 10, 12-13, 19, 20-21, 24, 25, 32, 32-33, 34-35, 36-37, 38-39, 42-43, 44-45, 46, 46-47, 48-49, 50a, 51, 52-53, 54, 56-57, 58-59, 60, 60-61, 62-63, 64, 65, 66-67, 68-69, 70, 70-71, 72-73, 74-75, 76, 76-77, 78, 79, 80, 80-81, 82-83, 84-85, 85, 86-87, 88, 88-89, 90-91, 91, 92-93, 94-95, 96, 96-97, 98, 100-101, 102-103, 104, 104-105, 106, 107, 108, 109, 110-111, 112-113, 116, 117, 118-119, 120-121, 121, 124, 124-125, 128-129, 130-131, 132, 134-135, 136-137, 139, 140-141, 142-143, 144-145, 146, 147, 148-149, 156-157, 158-159, 160, 161, 162-163, 164, 166
Osim Tsilum: 114, 150-151, 152-153, 153, 154-155
©Peter Harholdt/CORBIS, © 2002 Estate of Pablo Picasso/Artist Rights Society (ARS), New York: 41

Ramparts, Nimrod Fortress, Israel

Tel Aviv, 2000

This memoir begins with my husband, Ted, and my arrival
in Israel ten years ago. It is a story of the unexpected, a story that
portrays both my love for my husband and the love I developed for Israel.
Soon after I arrived in Israel, I began to write professionally about my
discoveries in this Mediterranean land. I then turned to Neil Folberg
to illustrate my narrative with his breathtaking photography.

Although Ted became critically ill after five years, the beginning of
the memoir does not reflect my sense of tragic loss. I chose instead to
retain the narrative chronology as it evolved because it enabled me to
show the reader a pattern of growth through discovery—and deep loss.

I dedicate this to the memory of my beloved husband,
Ted Arison (1924–1999).

Stone wall, Ein Kerem, Israel

CHAPTER ONE

Lost Love

Miami Gone

Returning to Miami, 1957: Accelerating across the arching span of Julia Tuttle Causeway, I am a kid from New York on a tropical ferris wheel…touching the sky and flying over the sea.

Leaving Miami, 1990: Ice-cream-colored, sun-drenched buildings are caressed by strains of Brahms played by bright-eyed, fresh-faced youths. Romantic cafés huddle under starry nights. Palm trees sway in the breeze. Expansive, blue, crystal-clear waters stretch out in every direction. . . .

From the very beginning I loved Miami, my home for thirty-five years. It was full of life and color—it was the place where I'd hoped to grow old. But much as I loved the city, I loved my husband more. We left because of Ted. And if truth be told, as painful as it was to leave Miami, moving felt familiar. After all, I come from a family that is mobile. My parents moved with me from New York, my birthplace, to Miami when I was two, to Boston when I was five, and back to New York when I was six. I think we lived in eight different residences during those few short

In the few childhood years I lived in Miami, I got "sand in my shoes" —I had to come back. I was even more fortunate to discover love there, although that love led me to a foreign land.

South Beach, Miami

© Corbis

Bayfront Park, Miami Beach

years. My mother, who claims she is a gypsy, never likes to stay in one place very long; to date, she has moved more than thirty times. After just a few years in a pleasant assisted-living environment, she is already restless. I am her daughter.

As an adult, I returned to Miami on the back of a motorcycle. Years later, I met my husband, Ted, also a gypsy. Born in Israel, he moved to New York and then to Miami, never staying in one spot for very long. There were always trips—often for business reasons— and he welcomed them. So did I.

Miami had been our home for all of our married life, and we had thrived there. By 1990, however, Ted needed a change. That year he had resigned as chairman of the board of Carnival Cruise Lines, completely turning over the very successful business he had created to his son, Micky, who had already been president of CCL for over a decade. Ted knew from experience when it was time to step down. In 1979, when he had asked Micky if he was ready to take over as president, Micky had wisely asked Ted if he was ready to let go. Forced to confront the reality of the situation, Ted quickly realized that Micky was right—he had to move out of the Carnival building and into an office somewhere else in Miami so that the executives wouldn't bypass Micky and come to him instead. The transition

had gone so well that Micky had soon turned Carnival into the world's largest cruise line.

Now, a decade later, Ted knew Micky was ready to take full control as chairman. But he wasn't prepared for the dramatic changes that occurred as a result. After the transfer of power took place, CCL no longer needed Ted. His three telephones stopped ringing. All the people in town who needed to contact CCL began calling Micky instead. Power is like water; it flows to the office of the chairman. No one entered Ted's large, high-ceilinged marble mausoleum of an office. His secretary worriedly confided to me that he would come out to her desk and ask plaintively, "Isn't there anything for me?" At lunchtime he would walk in Bayfront Park, aimlessly watching pigeons, vacantly staring into the windows of electronics stores on Flagler Street. Ted, the most energetic and creative of men, had turned into a shadow of his former self . . . and I was not in the market for a specter as a husband. With no purpose in his life, he was falling apart. What were we to do?

It was then that I overheard him wistfully telling a fellow Israeli expatriate that he would really like to move back to Israel. For years I had resisted his suggestion of having a second home in Israel, believing that it would eventually become our first. I felt that living in Israel, even on a limited basis, would be the first step

Directing our life came naturally to Ted. In fact, he gently directed everyone. Early in our marriage I rebelled against his self-assurance and constant movement, but eventually I learned to stand back and observed him impatiently prodding board chairmen as well. It wasn't because I was a woman, younger, or weaker that he was pushing me . . . it was just his way, so I stopped resisting.

toward getting swallowed by a foreign land. But now my husband was in real trouble. So despite my concerns, I wholeheartedly supported him.

Life with Ted had always been dramatic. Initially the drama included the wildest economic ups and downs: We met when he was down; then he was a success for a few years, and then down again, near bankruptcy, and losing our home, among other things. But we shared these difficult times—they only brought us closer.

Shortly after we married, when his business partnership had broken apart and he was left with a skeleton organization, very little money, and no ship, Ted called me to join him on a business trip in London. . . .

London

"Linnie," he said, "when you see the ship, don't look at the rust, don't look at the dirt, and don't look at the dowdy old English furniture."

"What am I to look at?" I wondered. "The possibilities?"

Ted assured me, "It's going to be the most beautiful ship in the world."

So I went to London, feeling hopeful. I wasn't surprised that Ted wanted me with him. We shared a wondrous closeness; in fact, we were always reaching out to each other. We were often holding hands and in doing so we found more than reassurance; there was a very real presence. I was part of everything he did. Hand-in-hand, he was there for me and I for him.

While he was trying to raise the money for our shipping business, I prowled the streets of London. It wasn't an easy time. One day I popped in to a movie theater to watch *A Clockwork Orange*. It seemed comedic. Years later, when I saw it again with friends, I was shocked at

its brutality. Our life had been so tumultuous and traumatic in those London days that the film, by comparison, had felt like a comedy.

Everything was difficult then. Even the hotel we were staying at suffocated me. Its black wallpaper pierced by green leafy vines was strewn with red and orange flowers that encased the dining room. With Ted immersed in his work, we had eaten dinner there every night for weeks. Finally one evening I begged my husband to walk down the street to find a little Italian restaurant so that we could take a breather. He did try. But as soon as we got a few steps away from the hotel, he looked so panic-stricken that I gently took his arm and walked him back. He had been waiting night and day for the telephone call that would announce he had the money to buy his first cruise ship.

When he finally succeeded in buying that ship and we were able to come home to Miami, I breathed a sigh of relief. "Now," I thought, "it'll be clear sailing." Was I in

I knew when I married an Israeli that it would lead to unexpected events because even in good marriages like ours, spouses have individual needs.

for a shock! On her maiden voyage the newly renamed *Mardi Gras* went aground on a sandbar right outside the port of Miami. This maritime fiasco made front-page news all over the world.

For years we struggled, unable to pay the bills. I wandered around Miami with my stomach in knots but trusted that Ted would find a way out. I believed in him. I knew someday he'd make it. Every night when he came home from work, I'd ask optimistically, "Well, how was it today?" After another grueling day, his answer was blunt: "I don't see a light at the end of the tunnel."

Yet gradually the light revealed itself. Our life became less frightening, and eventually the threatening shadows disappeared. Over the next four years, without our even noticing the moment of turnaround, Carnival Cruise Lines took off.

Tel Aviv

In our twenty-two years in Miami we had built a meaningful life together that would be painful to uproot. With Michael Tilson Thomas, we had created an academy of music, the New World Symphony orchestra. We founded the National Foundation for Advancement in the Arts (NFAA), an organization that encourages young artists in high schools nationwide. And to support our city, which had given us so much, we even started the Miami Heat, an NBA basketball team.

Neither one of us wished to surrender any of our interests in Miami. And though Ted was looking forward to the move, he wasn't sure how his return to Israel would be viewed. There is a national myth that people do not leave the new state, and he wondered, "Will the Israelis resent me?" At the time, I did not realize that Ted's return was so complicated. This fear—along with his general malaise—would diminish Ted's ability to bolster me in our new home.

My own concerns were simpler. First, I would be moving to a place without knowing the language. Despite having traveled to Israel many times, I had never learned Hebrew, because there had been no need to. As with all foreign businessmen who lived in the States, Ted spoke English well—he had no choice. Second, though I loved being with Ted's family and friends during our visits to Israel, I had never been attracted to the country. The air over Israel seemed to be a sandy haze that covered everything with a thin film of desert grit. Tel Aviv in particular struck me as a small, undeveloped town with repetitive rectangular apartment buildings, all decaying and crumbling. I lived in green, luscious Miami with its turquoise sea, large spaces, breathtaking views, and pastel Art Deco buildings. By comparison, Israel felt parched, as if it needed a bath and a long drink of water.

However, after much discussion, and given Ted's sensitivities and loyalties, we decided we could make this move work. With modern technology—even from such a distance—we believed we could keep the Miami connection. I also was determined to learn Hebrew.

And though I couldn't change the landscape, I could adjust. Finally, we agreed that if our move did not succeed, we could always return. We were very, very reasonable. . . . Of course, life proved to be less than reasonable. Whoever says reason and romance go together has never experienced romance!

In 1990 we bought two apartments in Tel Aviv—one almost completed, which would be our first residence, and one to be finished in five years, where we really wanted to live. In February 1991 we took off for Israel, stopping in London for a few days. Israel, in the middle of the Gulf War, was suffering Scud missile attacks. Ted offered me the option of our waiting out the war in London, but wars are always breaking out in Israel and as an incipient Israeli, I felt I could not run from them. As we flew into Israel, our plane was diverted from its usual flight pattern over the Tel Aviv coastline to avoid the potential Scuds. I should have known that this surreal arrival was emblematic of what I might expect in the future. I was not to be disappointed.

In Tel Aviv, feeling old and worn-out, Ted entertained visions of retiring. I was sure, however, that if he had no schedule to get him out of the house, he would sink into a deep depression. So I persuaded him to open an office.

"What will I do there?" he asked.

"Something will turn up," I assured him. I had no doubt that with his creativity, something *would* turn up. He was a natural risk-taker and not afraid of failure; still, in his weakened condition, it was quite painful for him to start over. We both felt at a loss in our new home.

Venice, Italy

Although it took some time—certainly over a year—eventually Ted entered the Israeli business scene in a big way. He introduced capitalism into Israel's socialistic banking, building, and development industries. He supplied risk capital for inventors and high-tech projects, and actively supported numerous charities. Finally back home with his family and childhood friends, he was speaking Hebrew, his native tongue. He continued building cruise ships for Carnival, much to Micky's delight, and he felt that he had embarked on one of the most fulfilling periods of his life. He solved his reentry to Israel by bringing his American expertise into the country, and as a result was beloved for his understated, charismatic leadership.

Ted had come full-circle . . . but I remained outside the circle, left far behind. I must admit this was mostly my own doing. Before we left Miami, a doctor had told me that I was a "service organization," critically referring to all the charity work I had done. Seeing that I had little sense of self, he had advised me to "do my own thing." So I was determined that when I came to Israel, I was not going to get hooked into doing anything until I found out what "my own thing" was, and then . . . do it. It had to be something new and special, something that I knew was a part of me but had not yet been developed. As a result, I kept myself separate from the many charitable and social activities that I could have joined.

At first, in spite of different time zones, we maintained contact with our charitable organizations in Miami. To develop an international support society for

View from Mount of Olives, Jerusalem

Fast-food menus in Hebrew

the New World Symphony, we flew to Madrid, Majorca, Venice, Paris, and Monte Carlo, where young musicians gave chamber music concerts in private villas. But eventually, because of illness, we had to give this up, and so we lost touch with a rich part of our previous life. Even though it was a relief to relinquish the responsibilities, the loss of these elements from my life made Miami seem farther away and made Israel seem more isolated.

But I was trying to assimilate. Immediately after the Gulf War, I attended an *ulpan*, a school designed to teach Hebrew to newcomers. The Russians, Bulgarians, Argentineans, and Italians seemed to speak Hebrew easily while we Americans had a much harder time. It was a struggle, but I wanted to learn. When I spoke my first hesitant Hebrew sentence to Ted, though, he irritably corrected my pronunciation. Mortified, I vowed never to speak Hebrew to him again. We had always enjoyed each other's company, and I didn't want to spoil it.

It was difficult, too, to get to class. Ted wanted me to accompany him on his business trips as I always had, and since I did not want to strain my marriage, I often skipped class. Then shortly after we arrived, Ted had an operation, and I left the *ulpan* to nurse him back to health. After several aborted attempts at finishing the *ulpan*, my resolve diminished. I dropped out. I tried private tutors, but we were in and out of the country so much that my focus on learning the language was completely destroyed.

I faced the reality that no matter how hard or long I devoted myself to learning Hebrew, I would never be able to speak it better than a child, and not a smart child at that. Since I'm a communicator, I chose to concentrate on English. Just about everyone in Israel speaks English, but that decision left me feeling less than fulfilled.

I suffered, knowing how much more effective I'd been for Ted in Miami, where language had not been an issue. There, it had been through communication that I'd helped develop a wide group of supporters to join in our endeavors. In Israel, I was still part of Ted's creations—we discussed his plans often, and I would encourage him—but I could not enable him in the same way I had in the States.

The language barrier also prevented me from attending even musical theater with my husband, because the songs were in Hebrew. And Ted was embarrassed that his wife did not speak the language, having been brought up in the pre-State days under the British Mandate with the national doctrine that everyone in Israel had to speak Hebrew.

Above Kinneret, Israel

At dinner at our home, Ted told our guests, "You can speak Hebrew, Lin understands."

"If you want me to understand," I countered, coloring, "you'll have to talk in English."

Our friends and associates complied, and eventually Ted got over his embarrassment when he saw how well I was accepted. Things had changed in Israel since he was a boy.

Still, I was tired of hearing a language I couldn't understand. I tried to hide my pain from Ted—I didn't want to add to his burdens—but occasionally he would glimpse my desperation, like the time he caught me screaming in frustration at the television because he had the news on in Hebrew. He couldn't help me because he had his hands full. In fact, he assumed that my usual optimism would encourage him. So I managed to put on a brave front, even to myself.

Ted's family and friends did everything in their power to make me feel at home. They were warm, loving, and resourceful, offering many suggestions to make my life more comfortable. But I was looking for something that no one could give me. I wanted to use my own voice, rather than Ted's, to create my own identity and exercise my autonomy. In Israel, I felt I'd lost myself. Without language, I was childlike and tongue-tied, living in a vacuum of understanding. Ted's life was flourishing, but mine seemed nonexistent.

About that time, Ted's daughter, Shari, her husband, and four of our grandchildren moved from Miami to Israel. We were close, but even they did not pry me out of my uncomfortable cocoon. In fact, their move only emphasized my linguistic isolation, since they all spoke Hebrew.

These feelings of loss and isolation reminded me of a long-forgotten experience from my earliest childhood. As a five-year-old, I'd been attached to a doll I named Sleepyhead. Sleepyhead had been my Linus blanket; I felt as if I could not live without her. When she became threadbare, my mother replaced Sleepyhead with a fresh new one, not realizing she had taken my best friend. I was devastated. I never looked at the new doll,

Nahal Tabor

but trailed along instead with a string attached to an invisible dog I called "Tivoli," named after a movie theater on Eighth Street. I told Tivoli all the secrets I had once reserved for the old Sleepyhead.

Like Sleepyhead, my beloved Miami had also been taken from me. There were differences, of course, between the two events: Sleepyhead had been taken from me because she was threadbare. Mother was right to remove Sleepyhead; she was falling apart and theoretically could be replaced. It was somewhat different this time. Miami was not threadbare for me—it was vibrant and alive. Every second of my life there was filled with purpose: family, friends, and work. For Ted, however, life in the city had come to a halt. So despite my love for Miami, I had left.

Losing my home and my language was extremely traumatic—much more so than losing a childhood doll. When I was young, I'd coped by creating an imaginary friend. But at the age of fifty-three, I was obviously too old for an invisible dog. And I could not move back to Miami—once Sleepyhead disappears, she's gone. Still, I was a survivor, and in my youth had learned a survival strategy with positive implications. In my confusion in Israel, I couldn't imagine what such a strategy might prove to be, but it did indeed materialize.

Ironically, I was to find my very own niche in Israel by leaving the country. Ted wanted us to cruise on our boat around the Galápagos Islands off the coast of Ecuador. I knew precious little about the Galápagos, but since I loved exploring, I was willing. At that point, escape was especially welcome.

Bayside Park in Miami

Evolutionary Development
à la Darwin

Bartolomé Island, Galápagos, Ecuador

About two years after our move to Israel, we vacationed in the Galápagos. On our cruise, some members of our family group began sketching sea lions and startling blue-footed boobies, tropical sea birds native to the islands. Initially I was not very impressed with the Galápagos, but the family's desire to create was contagious. Inspired by their doodling, I folded a large white sheet of drawing paper into quarters, filling all sides with my verbal impressions. As I wrote I realized what a strange and unique place we were visiting. Well-traveled friends, for instance, were overwhelmed with childlike wonderment when swimming with the sea lions. These friendly animals enticed us with their underwater antics, brushing their silky whiskers against our faces. And the birds did not fly away, no matter how close we got.

At home in Darwin's remarkable islands, I wrote of the tart made with edible flowers at Furio's restaurant; the blue-footed boobies whistling and parading their bright turquoise-blue webbed feet high in the air as they swooped from flight to land feetfirst in front of their

The Galápagos was a microcosm of flora and fauna, and it awakened my own excitement.

Iguana

proposed mates; antediluvian tortoises and iguanas; and the Mars-like islands of hardened lava that seemed to have come from another world.

Having poured out my excitement about the Galápagos, I wanted to share it. Once Ted and I returned home, I contacted the travel editor at the *Miami Herald*. He was interested in my story and suggested that I send along some photographs. All I had were what seemed to be normal vacation shots, but after they were printed with the story, they looked colorful and impressive. I was thrilled to see myself in print!

After my travel article was published, I thought about the many exciting places I had come across in Israel and wondered whether I could write about them as well, sharing my discoveries with others. I knew that even our friends from Miami—who often visited Israel, staying in hotels—had no idea what treasures were hidden throughout the countryside. Most Israelis took affluent tourists to the expected locations and not to the nooks and crannies that I had chanced upon. Chic restaurants, for example, had sprouted in decayed neighborhoods of Tel Aviv, and only a local like me would know about them. With some trepidation, I sent my newspaper article about the Galápagos to some writer-friends to see whether they felt I could develop into a serious writer.

Sarah Arison

Lin Arison

"Go for it," they assured me.

So I did. And my subsequent personal evolution—spurred by my writing—was no less exciting to me than Darwin's.

I had written before. When I had arrived in Miami at age twenty—on the back of my first husband's motorcycle—I became a legal secretary while my husband went to college on the G.I. Bill. Soon after, I was appointed publicity chairman of the Miami Legal Secretaries Association, where I was a member. I had no idea what a publicity chairman did, however, so I went to the club editor of each of the newspapers in town to ask for pointers. They taught me how to write releases, and thereafter the legal secretaries received an abundance of publicity.

The job was a turning point for me. In fact, the day my first husband walked out on our three-year-old son, Michael, and me, I had been sent home with a typewriter to provide information about the legal secretaries for one of the columnists of the *Miami Review*. I arrived, expecting my husband to help me inside with the heavy manual typewriter that was in the trunk of our car. Instead I walked in to find his farewell note on a legal-size yellow pad. Since we'd never argued, I laughed, thinking he was playing a joke on me. I even looked for him in the closets!

After the shock had subsided around two in the morning, I sat down to write the legal secretarial news. The article naturally formed itself into a beginning, middle, and an end. I dropped the piece off at the *Miami Review* office that morning on my way to work, and within an hour the publisher called to say he was giving me a daily column of my own in his legal newspaper. It saved my life—or at least my sanity. My first husband may have abandoned me, but I was a writer and was worth something. I had a special skill inside me that I hadn't known was there. I had been abandoned, but not destroyed.

This gave me the courage to take risks. I soon left my secure nine-to-five legal secretarial job to do all-hours public relations for the owner of a children's theater. I knew I needed to learn more about the profession, so I asked an acquaintance whether I could work for her firm without pay just for the experience. She said this would be too disruptive, but advised me to approach the head of public relations at Tropical Race Track for a job.

He was direct. "Have you written about society before?"

"No."

"Do you know anything about horses or racing?"

"No," I answered, beginning to feel ridiculous.

He studied me for a moment. "Are you willing to jump into the pool and see whether you can swim?"

"Most definitely, yes."

I arrived at the racetrack the next morning before dawn. The stables smelled of hay, manure, leather, and the nervous sweat on the horses' hides. I walked up to the trainers and introduced myself. They were surprised that someone who worked in the Turf Club had come so early in the morning to see what they were doing with the horses. I confessed to them that I knew nothing about racing but was expected to write as if I did. My method was to learn from the inside out—the inside being the

Nahal Srach, Galilee

stables where the stories would begin. The trainers kindly took me under their wing; leaning on the railing as they clocked their horses, they told me scuttlebutt about the owners. Later in the day, with butterflies in my stomach, I entered the Turf Club, where the ushers, who became my guardian angels, touted me as to which of the owners would provide the best story material. Although the horses were very nice, my articles about the racetrack tended to be human interest pieces, and with pictures taken by the track photographer, they regularly ended up in the sports section of the newspaper.

After a season of this, I started working in a regular public relations firm, but quickly realized I needed to give up my frenetic pace to provide a more stable routine for my son, who was now five. One of my firm's clients was Arison Shipping Co., and their vice president was looking for a secretary. I was ready to go back to a nine-to-five job. It was while I was working there that, as Ted often told our friends, he fell in love with my smile.

Upon returning to Israel after the Galápagos vacation, I asked a cousin of Ted's who was an editor to

Nahal Beit Ha'emek, Israel

help me find a writing job. He introduced me to two editors and, after reading the Galápagos article, they asked me to work for them. One translated the article into Hebrew and put it into a travel magazine sent to seventy thousand Gold Visa cardholders in Israel. He also translated the stories I wrote about a subsequent cruise to Polynesia and then to the Yucatán, as well as a trip to Canyon Ranch Spa in Arizona.

The other editor asked me to write a monthly column for a business magazine called *Link*, published and sold in Israel and also mailed to the United States, England, Japan, India, and even the Arab countries. "Exploring with Lin" suggested foods, menus, and restaurants along with fascinating places off the beaten path to visit when coming to Israel on business trips. Just as with the Galápagos article, I took my own photographs. I described the Galilee from my first trip in a ranger's open jeep, the dust of the road covering my Louis Vuitton luggage. In the neighborhood off Rothschild Boulevard where Ted grew up and Meir Dizengoff, the first mayor of Tel Aviv, had his home, I wrote about a restaurant where the freshly grilled salmon is delicious. Subsequently, Dizengoff's home became the first Tel Aviv museum and also was where David Ben-Gurion signed the Declaration of the State of Israel in 1948, just one day before five Arab nations invaded the fledgling state.

I salivated, too, over the fare served in the Keren Restaurant, located in an authentically renovated wood-and-stone home in the American Colony in Jaffa, the old port of Tel Aviv. In the same neighborhood, Baron Platon von Ustinov, the grandfather of actor Peter Ustinov, had established a zoo, an archaeological museum, and a twenty-three-bed hospital.

I also described Mitzpe Ramon, a crater of pink and turquoise striations that I traversed with my guide, David Perlmutter, in his jeep, as well as the prehistoric desert mountains five minutes from downtown Eilat, where we climbed over what looked like tiramisu cliffs and marshmallow and hot fudge ripples. David provided me with scientific explanations for these colors and formations, but being food oriented, I preferred my own. The reader received the benefit of both David's science and my appetite. As I gathered information, I found myself reveling in the simple luxury of coming out of the bright desert sunlight and sitting in the cool shade under a rocky ledge. A drink of icy water after sweaty hiking was more exciting to me than diamonds. As I traveled and gathered tidbits for my column, I gained confidence and began to tour alone in my own car. I found myself searching instinctively for elements that reminded me of my previous Mediterranean travels and, invariably, I found them.

Waking up in the morning became a joy instead of bleak depression. I couldn't wait to drive onto the open road to face the surprises that awaited me. Part of my happiness was in tasting food. I now had the perfect excuse not to diet. I was exploring, and exploring to me meant food as well as history. I put on too much weight, but at least I was happy again and better educated.

Lake Kinneret, Poriya, Israel

CHAPTER THREE

Exploration and Discovery
The Open Road

Increasingly, my search for articles took me outside of Tel Aviv. I welcomed the escape. The city intimidated me. Tel Aviv was a small, closely knit town where everyone seemed to know each other. The Israelis there were serious, intelligent people who always appeared productive and purposeful. Even the way they gathered at cafés seemed sophisticated to me. In contrast, I had no serious purpose as of yet, no clear-sighted commitment. I was just floating along, trying to feel good. I didn't want anyone to know how rootless I felt.

I was curious about my new country and wanted to learn all I could about it, perhaps in hopes of discovering my place in it.

Besides, Tel Aviv was unattractive. Built over a half century earlier, its dirty stucco was crumbling back into the sand dunes from which it had come. Compared to the beauty I was used to in Miami, I felt I was stuck in an ugly place. By running away—and exploring—I could escape from both the city and myself.

When I was a small child, before I understood such romance, the open road was already surreptitiously calling me and imprinting its mark. I remembered how as a young adult, driving over

Ancient synagogue in Navoria, Israel

the bridge that spanned the Miami River, my tires had strummed a startling song of recognition as they coursed over the grating of the bridge. I'd held the steering wheel tightly as I picked through a file of memories to recall the sleepy three-year-old lying on her belly, feet tucked up into a protective ball, eyes closed and sweaty body pressed against the coarse fabric of the back-seat. The windows of the car must have been open as there was no air conditioning in those days, and the heat of the pavement baked the tires as they sped along. Through a sodden semi-sleep, the thrumming noise lasted just a few moments but fixed itself in my childhood memory . . . and then returned abruptly many years later, when I again drove across the Miami Avenue Bridge.

The memory reminded me of my childhood home of so many years ago, the old Miami of 1940 without air con-dition ing. The humidity was so thick that my father couldn't get dry after he took a shower—he felt he couldn't breathe. Eventually he dragged my mother and me back to New York. But the thrum of the road had taken hold and has remained with me ever since.

As a young teenager in New York, I would escape the confines of our one-bedroom apartment by climbing onto a bus at 175th Street, headed for the Metropolitan Museum of Art on Fifth Avenue. Later in the day, I would prowl through Greenwich Village. Sitting at the front of the bus near the driver, I'd watch

Sanibel Beach, Florida

everything we passed in the city but occasionally would fix my gaze on the road's white dividing line. It was mesmerizing. To this day, the painted white-ribboned line and the aroma of diesel fuel from a bus's exhaust still give me a rush of anticipation.

Years later, as a divorcée, I found myself again heeding the call of the road after watching a drive-in movie with my three-year-old son, Michael, asleep on a pillow in the backseat of the car. As the lot emptied, I couldn't bear to return to my lonely house and my familiar but empty routines. Desperate for a change of scene in the middle of the night, I decided to pack up our bathing suits and a few clothes and begin the slow, entranc-ing drive to the shell beach of Sanibel on the west coast of Florida. Sitting on the sand with Michael playing in the surf, I took up my pen, and the poetry poured forth. I can still hear the sound of the waves pounding the beach in a rhythmic cadence.

When Ted and I moved to Monaco in the late 1970s, I faced a similar emptiness during the day while he was in his shipping office. The few friends we had were not enough. I didn't belong, and worse, I felt my life had no purpose in this sophisticated principality where the language was strange and the lifestyle formi-dable. To escape, I would drop Ted off at his office and take to the open road. Clutching the wheel safely in hand suggested that I had some control over my life.

Facing the open road early in the morning was like my choosing hot fudge sundaes in my early teens when I was reed thin, or the movies on a Saturday after-noon; it was the freedom to experience what-ever lay ahead.

I cruised through small villages in the south of France, following the inviting cobblestones to find whatever lay around the corner. Nothing was planned; my day was full of surprises.

I had my cappuccino as I watched a postman lean against the wooden bar of the café in order to throw back his early-morning cognac. I drove to Vallauris and visited the Madoura atelier, where Picasso learned to make his ceramics. Picasso had taken the red clay amphora and by hand molded it into a woman's body, or perhaps a bird's, then added the enamel, which turned into glaze upon firing. The Madoura gallery now sells copies of Picasso's ceramics, his plates slashed with black bullfighters and their enraged opponents, snorting and pawing the bullrings that he frequented in Arles and Nîmes.

Vallauris reverberates with the strong life of Picasso and Françoise Gilot and their two children, Claude and Paloma. Their former villa, La Galloise, is still perched high in the hills above the town. It was in Vallauris that I first bought some fish dishes designed by Roger Charpon, red clay covered with thick white glaze, a turquoise ring around the edges, each encircling in its center a different turquoise fish of the Midi. Today I use these plates in my apartment in Israel, and they bring back memories of Monaco

Picasso plates

dinners of grilled sea bass with dried fennel, and our light wooden table surrounded by Knoll chairs covered with woven cream cushions.

While living in Monaco, I also drove to the chapel in nearby Vence, with its white walls broken by black line drawings. The only light in the chapel shone through an expansive stained-glass window. To me, the light appeared startling blue, but upon further reflection I am not so sure: I remember that Françoise Gilot wrote in her book *Life with Picasso* that Matisse combined a blue, green, and yellow Tahitian motif in the stained glass, hoping that each color would retain its vibrancy. She and Picasso, however, felt that Matisse failed because the resulting light came out instead a dull pink mauve "that resembled a bathroom." Although I cherish the striking blue I retain in my mind's eye, one day I will go back to reexamine the chapel.

Down the road from the chapel, in the square in front of the Hotel Colombe d'Or in St. Paul de Vence—after a lunch of hors d'oeuvres and crudités—I stood and watched Yves Montand play boule. Close by on a bench sat acclaimed actress Simone Signoret, rotund but majestic, with shining gray hair and wise eyes. Behind the Colombe d'Or a green valley strewn with red poppies beckoned, reminding me of Monet's *Les*

Coquelicots and Renoir's *Path Through High Grass*. I wrote many letters to friends describing these villages and my picturesque automotive adventures. They allowed me to flee from my loneliness into the bright sunshine of green meadows and scarlet flowers.

In Israel, however, it was not so easy to explore. At first I was too busy. Trying to learn the language, I spent five hours a day, five days a week at the *ulpan*—with three hours of homework every day. Then, after I dropped out, I was afraid to drive for fear that I would get lost. I had not been afraid of losing my way in France, but the possibility of getting lost in Israel frightened me. I couldn't read the signs in Hebrew as I whizzed by, and besides, it was a small country with dangerous borders.

So I explored with English-speaking guides. Into the open countryside I went in search of information for my travel articles for *Link*. Although I was dependent on someone else, I had returned to the open road. This time I would bring home more than glazed clay dishes to be used on our dinner table. Although I was not certain of my own story, I would bring back the stories of the land. I was focused and constructively engaged as a reporter because I had left myself—and my life in Tel Aviv—far behind, in search of unexpected discoveries. I followed my instincts and my curiosity to find people and places that interested me. The bond I would form with these people and places—winemakers and restaurateurs, villages and cafés—would eventually enable me to reemerge, to rediscover myself. And so it was when I stumbled on Rosh Pina in the Upper Galilee. . . .

Ancient olive press, Danela, Israel

Sycamore tree near the Jordan River

CHAPTER FOUR

Rosh Pina

Climbing the Hill

Serendipity must have been working overtime the day I came upon Rosh Pina. I was on my way to visit the artists' village of Safed in the Upper Galilee when my guide suggested that we peek in at the one at Rosh Pina as well. Eagerly, I agreed. I stared out the window with anticipation as our car seemed to climb straight up a cypress-lined road, passing charming bed-and-breakfasts in weathered stone houses, their terra-cotta roofs inundated with pink geraniums and bright orange bougainvillea. The combination of old stone and brilliant flowers immediately reminded me of the hills of Provence. The paved street ended abruptly at a barrier to a narrow cobblestone lane, and we pulled into an adjacent dirt parking lot.

When I opened the car door, I was dizzy with delight. The birds were singing, and the air smelled fresh and radiant. I asked my guide to wait a moment while I looked around. Following the steep winding cobblestones, I walked up to the oldest part of town. I became characteristically caught up in my wanderings

After spending time with the people and land of Rosh Pina, I knew for the first time I could live successfully in Israel.

and lost all sense of time. Ted never liked to join me on my forays, and I could understand why. He wanted to know how long it would take to get to our destination, how long we would be there, and when we would be back home. I could never answer him; when I explore, I never know what's going to happen. Who could have predicted when I took off from Tel Aviv early that morning that I was going to fall in love with Rosh Pina later that day?

Rosh Pina was in shambles, and immediately I loved the town because

View of Mt. Hermon from Marut

of it. Some of my favorite places—Greenwich Village, Coconut Grove, and South Beach, for example—were all a mess when I first discovered them. Like a child's kaleidoscope of colorful fragments constantly moving by happenstance into different shapes and configurations, unfinished places are beautiful, full of possibilities. There is a freedom in disorder; it is without limits or boundaries. Once a place is orderly, it is contained, inert—and for me, it lacks romance.

I surveyed the small crumbling lanes of Rosh Pina with pleasure. Before me stretched linear low stone ruins atop the cobblestone hill. Orange and yellow

wildflowers climbed high behind the empty facades of roofless buildings, which a century ago had housed almost thirty Romanian pioneer families living cramped together with their livestock. The crumbling stones, jagged and white, stood out in sharp relief against the stark blue sky. I felt I was on top of the world, but considerably more barren and rocky mountains rose above the old village. Safed was nowhere in sight, and it was just as well. I would visit it another time. I assumed it must lie on the other side of the mountain, and I was quite happy to be on this side.

Toward the end of the street I came to a run-down one-room synagogue, where someone was chanting Hebrew in a singsong cadence. Looking through the window, I saw a tall, lanky middle-aged man gesturing enthusiastically to a group of rapt youngsters. He was wearing a brown cowboy hat with a tooled leather band, and from underneath it poked a few strands of straight blond hair that straggled over his ears. With his piercing blue eyes and skillful storytelling, he held the students' attention.

My life with Ted always felt limitless. Surrounded by construction and creation, we were constantly moving, living in perpetually changing edifices and environments. Dust and jackhammers had been our companions for most of our life together. Homes, ships, hotels, apartment buildings, offices … all were in some stage of creation. All were in motion.

Arik the storyteller, Rosh Pina

Rosh Pina

Farther down the hill I peeked into the artists' studios, tucked into renovated stone houses along the last part of the curved lane. Painters, jewelers, and pottery makers worked industriously, leading me to believe I was not the only one who felt comfortable in this lovely, ramshackle place.

Crossing the lane, I spotted the impressive two-story remains of the old Schwartz Hotel. Rickety wooden scaffolding braced the hotel ruin. Without a roof, the structure was filled with clear blue sky that shone brilliantly through its windows. Next to the hotel was a quaint lean-to, where a leathersmith worked. Curious, I peeked in and introduced myself. Micha, the leathersmith, brewed me a steaming mug of tea made from local herbs he had collected from the hillsides. As I sat sipping, he continued to tool leather straps like the one I'd seen embellishing the story-teller's hat brim. Comforted by Rosh Pina's quiet, controlled pace, I noticed the worn drums sitting on a shelf in Micha's workshop. Micha informed me that on weekends he and his friends make music in front of his lean-to or at a nearby restaurant located on a hill just under the art gallery on Pioneer Street. I hoped someday I would hear their music at one of their venues.

Several minutes later, the storyteller I'd noticed earlier entered the lean-to, and Micha introduced us. Arik—part of an organization of storytellers committed to keeping the oral traditions alive—had just finished instructing the schoolchildren in the synagogue and had dropped by to visit Micha. His walking stick intrigued me. On it he had carved the head of Abraham, father of the tribe; a ram; and Hopsa, the Bedouin, a mother figure. Arik uses his totemic staff as a prop for some of his stories, and had already worn out three of them.

Arik's own story was fascinating. As a twelve-year-old, he had fled from Poland with his family and moved to Israel. Living in stifling quarters in Tel Aviv, he had suffered the Israeli pressure to give up his Polish identity. In those early days of insecure mono-lithic Israel, he was not permitted to live in both worlds. For years Arik was constantly angry, unable to mask his bitterness toward his new country. Finally, however, he realized it would be easier if he emptied his head of comparisons by numbing his feelings to his Polish past. He lived on, feeling dead inside, until one day he happened to visit a friend in Rosh Pina. When Arik smelled bread baking in the mother's kitchen, all his stifled feelings burst forth. The comforting, homey smell made him feel human again—and for the first time, comfortable in Israel. Overcome with yearning, he walked outside and saw buds on the trees under an incandescent blue sky. Filled with wonder and well-being, he rejoiced in the knowledge that he had come alive.

Like his own story, most of Arik's historical tales were ones of overcoming hardship, of courage in the face of adversity. They reminded me of the fairy tales I'd heard as a child, where dangers were met head-on and dragons slain. I listened to Arik's stories with the same pleasure that I had experienced from my mother's bedtime tales. One of his stories in particular resonated

Kinneret Promenade, Rosh Pina

with me—the creation of Rosh Pina's old silk factory. Years ago, Arik related vividly, a large stationary steam engine for the silk factory had arrived by train all the way from the Gare du Nord in Paris to the edge of the landlocked Sea of Galilee. The steam engine was floated on a pontoon to the western shore at the bottom of the hills below Rosh Pina, and was then pushed and pulled upward by a determined group of villagers and their mules.

The story reminded me of one of my favorite tales, *The Little Engine That Could.* In it, the tiny engine would say, "I think I can. I think I can," as he attempted to climb over the mountain. *The Little Engine That Could* had a successful journey, and Rosh Pina's old steam engine made it up its own mountain as well. After months of pushing, it was ensconced in the silk factory building. Despite the villagers' valiant efforts, however, the silk factory failed because of insufficient

markets, and the town fell into decline. But not all was lost. Though the steam engine disappeared, the trail that it left behind—leading to the defunct silk factory and the failed winery—ironically became the village's first road from the Sea of Galilee.

Arik led me to the cinema and café that used to house the silk factory, and then to the community center, where the winery had been. We then walked to the town's pottery studio, once the center for renewing the Hebrew language. Unfortunately, that project's remarkable, almost miraculous success has so far not included me!

"Where were the mulberry trees planted to feed the silkworms?" I asked, still marveling at the town's unexpected historical roots.

He gestured, "You're leaning on one of them."

I looked up to discover an umbrella of dark green leaves that had once provided a veritable feast for the hapless silkworms. So much, it seemed, had disappeared from the town's past—but evidence of its industrial and cultural roots was still everywhere.

Indeed, Rosh Pina inspires hope . . . and romance. Of Arik's tales, my favorite was the love story that indirectly led to Rosh Pina's present renewal. This story, too, included parcels, arrivals, and indirection.

⌣

In the nineteenth century, Alter Schwartz started a small post office on the site of the now-crumbling Schwartz Hotel. A pair of donkeys carried the mail to and from Safed, and when the townspeople heard the

I had entered upon an adventure from which escape was not so easy...

clip-clop of the donkeys' hooves, they would call out, "Here comes the mail train!"

Carrying the mail was no easy task. Only a fearless man was able to outwit the Bedouin highwaymen lying in wait and thereby provide safe passage for the letters, artisans' tools, and silk produced in Baron Edmond de Rothschild's silk factory. Schwartz succeeded, though, and the baron's men rewarded him by helping him build an additional story to his post office, turning it into a hotel.

One day after finishing a small building project in Rosh Pina, a young pioneer, Reuven Yosef Paicovitch, was climbing the road to Safed to look for another job. His eyes met those of Haya Schwartz, who was accompanying her father, Alter, down the hill. Reuven immediately fell in love. Quickly he turned around to follow the girl and her father back down into the village, where he appeared on the family's doorstep.

"I want to marry your daughter," he addressed Schwartz.

Both Schwartz and his daughter admired Paicovitch's astonishing nerve. "If you will settle down and buy a piece of land," said Haya, "I'll consider it."

Baron de Rothschild's garden in Rosh Pina

Eager to prove his worthiness, Reuven did as she suggested. And a few years later, the marriage took place.

The young family became legendary in Rosh Pina. Haya and Reuven's youngest son, Yigal Allon, became a distinguished and celebrated Israeli military commander and statesman. As minister of labor, Allon enabled Rosh Pina to rebuild some of the small cottages that now house the settlers' museum and the artists' galleries that are sprouting along the cobblestone.

Coincidentally, Arik was working in Allon's ministry in Tel Aviv when he saw an ad in the newspaper looking for a storyteller for Rosh Pina. Recalling the aroma of bread baking and the fateful emotions it evoked stimulated him to answer the ad, and he returned to the place where he had come to life. Arik knows that his stories are helping renew Rosh Pina and is pleased that his personal destiny has become part of the town's rejuvenation.

When we arrived back at Micha's lean-to, something improbable occurred. As if from offstage, Merek Israel—Reuven Paicovitch's great-grandson—shyly shuffled into the leathersmith's workshop. In a village

of less than one thousand inhabitants, everyone knows each other's business. Realizing that Arik was telling stories about his great-grandfather, Merek joined us. He added that when Yigal Allon's mother died, Yigal, a six-year-old orphan, had been taken in by Merek's grandmother and had lived at the hotel for several months.

A cactus in Nahal Meshushim, Israel

"With such an auspicious history, do you think the hotel will be restored?" I asked Micha.

He shrugged sadly. "Probably, but that will mean I'll have to move."

Fortunately, Micha has been able to stay put for now. When I returned to Rosh Pina six months later, I saw that the lean-to still existed, and an official village signpost read "Micha, the leathersmith." It's likely that someday the Schwartz Hotel will be restored, but I am confident Rosh Pina will still have a place for Micha—after all, the leathersmith's sign is now hewn in stone.

Rosh Pina and its people touched me deeply. I'd already been there several hours and still felt I had much to explore. I said good-bye to my new friends and wandered down the cobblestone lane, where I saw my guide searching for me. Bored with waiting in the car, he was curious to see what I was up to. Having traveled with me before, he was not at all surprised that I was so immersed in Rosh Pina.

At the bottom of the lane, we joined a group of visitors who were entering the tiny museum of Rosh Pina. The museum had been created from the small stone home of Professor Gideon Mer, who, at the beginning of the twentieth century, had worked doggedly to combat the malaria that had plagued the early settlers. We soaked in the small town's history, even crawling under the house to see its earthen caves. Legend had it that Jews had hidden in these caves in the first century—almost two thousand years ago—during the unsuccessful Bar Kochba rebellion.

The first time I had tasted coupe marron was in Paris. Ted had ordered it, but I was on such a strict diet that I only dipped my spoon in and took one small bite. To this day I regret that restraint, because whenever coupe marron appears on a menu, I must taste and compare. There, in tiny Rosh Pina, I atoned for not eating the whole thing in Paris. I had learned the wisdom of desserts.

More recently, Baron Edmond de Rothschild had used these caves to store wine from his ill-fated enterprise. Revered as a great philanthropist, the baron had come to Israel in the late nineteenth century to restart the wine industry, and though he had succeeded famously in the village of Zichron Yaacov, he had not been as successful in Rosh Pina.

The intense history was overwhelming, and we were ready for a break. It was now lunchtime, and my guide, who also appreciated good food, suggested the nearby Dubrovin Farms for their smoked meat specialties. Ten minutes later we entered the settlement of Yesod Hama'alah in the Hula Reserve, where Gadi and Leah Berkuz introduced us to their marvelous menu. We decided to taste a bit of everything: smoked duck and trout, goose liver on skewers, spareribs, and grilled portobello mushrooms with goat cheese. For dessert I had coupe marron—candied chestnuts on homemade vanilla ice cream. It was delectable.

I had fallen in love with Rosh Pina, and now wished to share it with my beloved. Since I had already explored the town—and thus could tell him exactly what he would be experiencing—I knew Ted would be enthusiastic about joining me. The following winter we spent a weekend at Auberge Shulamit, an intimate four-room inn. The Berkuz family, who owned the inn, had moved from Dubrovin Farms to Rosh Pina itself, where they had transformed a historic three-story stone guesthouse, Auberge Shulamit, into a romantic lodging. Again, I was fascinated by the history of the home. In the nineteenth century, Shulamit's husband had been brought from Damascus to supervise the baron's silk factory. The inn had also been the site where the negotiations that ended the War of Independence on the Syrian front had taken place.

It was a magical time. Ted and I took brisk walks on country roads, slept under soft duvets at night, and ate chestnut soup and peppersteak in the glassed-in terrace of the Berkuzes' restaurant overlooking snowcapped Mount Hermon. When the terrace was full, the crowd spilled over into the Auberge's charming Provençal dining room with its wood-burning fireplace.

Rosh Pina was, indeed, being renewed. While on our trip, we discovered that the natural caves under the museum had recently been lined with stones—turning

Fields near the Kinneret, Israel

the baron's wine cellars into a continental restaurant. The natural gothic vaults caught the flickering glow of candlelight, making our dinner even more romantic. We shared an empanada filled with beef fillet as an appetizer, and then I had spring lamb while Ted had fresh salmon, both baked in clay casseroles. For dessert his choice was crêpe suzette, while mine was a delicate "drunken" pear cooked in red wine and drizzled with chocolate mint sauce. The twinkling lights in the valley below reminded me of dining alfresco in Monte Carlo with its glittering ground cover. In fact, we overlooked a scene no less romantic: the baron's perfumed and manicured French garden, surrounded by hundred-year-old cypress trees.

Ted was surprised at the changes he found in Rosh Pina. He had left a very provincial Israel in 1952. At that time, Saint Peter's fish was the only entrée offered on the shores of the Sea of Galilee, and as for cuisine en route, travelers made do with shabby places that served up hummus, tahini, and skewers of meat. Now, back in Israel after so many years, Ted was finding aesthetically pleasing international restaurants in places such as tiny Rosh Pina!

"This could be anywhere," he declared in amazement. Pleased, I smiled at Ted. So I was not dreaming after all. I had stumbled upon a very special place.

The long drive back to Tel Aviv unfortunately put Rosh Pina out of my spontaneous reach, but I knew that others would soon discover it. Its proximity to the lakeside town of Tiberias and the ski resort of Mount Hermon would ensure ample visitors. I, on the other hand, would have to plan my visits and could not just drop in.

Cave in Nahal Hazor, Israel

CHAPTER FIVE

Return to Rosh Pina

The Cornerstone Is Set

I t was spring when I finally found my way back to Rosh Pina. I'd wanted to stay overnight and since all the inns were full, someone kindly made arrangements for me in a private home. The cozy loft attached to Hana Eden's home was buried in the familiar bowers of bougainvillea at the top of the cobblestone hill. Hana welcomed me with a glass of delicious water from the tap. It tasted so pure, it was like drinking from an icy stream in the Catskill Mountains of my childhood.

"Where else in the world," I mused silently, "would you delight to drink tap water?"

In no time at all, I began to visualize turning the old stone ruin next door into a writing studio. It was quiet and isolated, covered by a blanket of trees, its air redolent with jasmine and honeysuckle. But, I soon realized, it was too far away from Tel Aviv and Ted would never visit; such solitude would engulf and drown me. Besides, a year spent supervising renovations instead of writing would not be practical. So reluctantly I surrendered the idea after a few days. Though I often return to

A Rosh Pina proverb says that if you drink the water, you will come back.

Rosh Pina as a visitor, secretly I wish I could live there.

After getting settled, I went exploring. A stone staircase led me down the hill behind Hana's house into her minuscule garden. Peering into a cave beneath her compound, I saw an ancient stone olive press, shining white against the eerie blackness. Then I crossed through a cluster of thick-trunked fig trees, came to a green wooden door in a fence at the end of the garden, and threw it open. In front of me lay an enchanting vista: Nahal Rosh Pina, a deep gorge of verdant foliage overgrown with purple morning glories, spread majestically before the undulating slopes of Mount Canaan. I tried to catch my breath. The sun was setting behind the mountains, casting the silk sky in pinks, purples, and deep blues. Settling on the cool grass, I watched it go.

Nahal Rosh Pina

I was alone, and all was quiet. Shadows fell on the mountains, and I let the silent darkness embrace me. Time passed quickly, without my realizing it. And then, limply, I returned to the warm yellow light of the bulbs in the loft, glowing on my travel case. I lifted out my toothbrush and set it on the glass shelf over the sink. I had found a special place, and its powers captivated me.

The next day on my morning walk, I discovered that the breathtaking Nahal Rosh Pina could also be seen from the Baron Stables restaurant, where Baron de Rothschild had kept his horses. The gorge ran behind the artists' studios and along the synagogue. On the hillside across the gorge I could see an old cemetery; on closer inspection I noted that some of the gravestones dated back at least one hundred years. Measured against Israel's ancient life span, one century is but a speck in time—and yet it seemed to me that the hardships and deaths experienced by the founding settlers of this hillside village occurred a long time ago. . . .

I entered Pina Barosh, one of the inns nearby, famous for Nili Friedman's breakfast: delicious diced tomato and cucumber salad, homemade cheeses, olives, marvelous fresh bread, and an omelet of onions and herbs made from the inn's farm-fresh eggs. The restaurant is very much a family venture. Nili's husband is a farmer—just like his great-grandfather so many years before, who founded Rosh Pina with his esrog and citron plantation for the religious settlers of Safed. Nili's sister, Amira Rubin, bakes the bread, makes the cheese, and gathers the olives and herbs.

Nili's daughter, Shiri, is the resident chef. She studied French cooking with Bernard Loiseau in Bourgogne, France, and also apprenticed at Daniel Boulud's restaurant in New York before returning to

Nili Friedman's bed-and-breakfast and Shiri Friedman's gourmet restaurant

Mark Rubin in Rosh Pina

Rosh Pina to open her own gourmet restaurant in the glassed-in addition over the breakfast nook in her family's inn. Shiri is constantly creating. Her savory double lamb chop floats on a sauce that changes according to the inspiration of the chef. Depending on the season, her entrecôte may be accompanied by red wine and butter, figs with mushrooms, or even orange and mandarin. In contrast, her desserts remain traditional with an excellent crème brûlée, chocolate terrine with cardamom, and pecan pie. And in fig season, the fruit is wrapped in filo dough and covered in crushed mango.

I sat at the small table, savoring my meal—and tried to get my mind off dessert. After all, it was only breakfast! Sipping my coffee, I took in the scenery. The quaint breakfast cove under the farmhouse overlooked a miniature ranch, with a small corral of cows and horses surrounded by lacy mimosa trees.

After breakfast I walked down the hill to the Rubins' rustic home and found myself in the midst of

Clouds in Nahal Dishon, Israel

olive trees, white goats, a brown mare, and Amira's black colt. As I stood before a gleaming white-tiled dairy and bakery, Amira—her rust-colored hair clasped in a pencil-thin braid encircling her head—approached me warily as a cat. Sensing that I would not disrupt the harmony of the household, she bid me welcome. I sat in front of the cutting board, watching her slice green apples into exact slivers, slip them into doughy crusts, and pop them into a large oven.

I also visited Amira's husband, Mark, in the family's barn, trading the aroma of baking for the fragrance of freshly mown hay. His head wrapped in an improbable white turban, Mark—a goatherd from Chicago—opened the corral and "yuhah'd" the goats into the milking shed. With each spurt of rhythmic milking came the frothy whiteness of the goats' milk. I was beguiled by the silent, rich, reflective beauty. Soon one of their young daughters, wearing her backpack, descended downhill through the green pastures filled

*Even now as I recall the wonderment of Rosh Pina, I do so with
trepidation, feeling that examining it in the light of day will make it disappear.
It was years before I could write about it professionally.*

with poppy-colored anemones. Farther up the hill I saw another girl—also saddled with a backpack—wending her way through the high grass in the same direction. It was as if in the soft light of morning, Monet's *Les Coquelicots* and Renoir's *Path Through High Grass* had come to life in the Galilee.

Amira and Mark's hillside is also a retreat for Beon, a sculptor. Beon forms limestone into sensual organic shapes. When I visited him, he spoke anxiously of the village's plan to build a road through the meadow that is his backyard. So far it is only talk. But Rosh Pina is changing, and there are no guarantees. Curiously, Beon, who lives and works in a plastic tent behind the corral, chose to sculpt in an extremely durable medium. His sculptures are practically indestructible. One piece I purchased fell out of my photographer Neil's van during a photo shoot. Weeks later on his family's holiday, Neil found it safely propped up by the side of the road. He dragged it back into his van, and it is now in my Tel Aviv home, no worse for wear.

The landscape of this small village felt familiar—and it brought me a great deal of comfort. Rosh Pina means "cornerstone" in Hebrew, and for me it became the center for the Mediterranean flavors, colors, aromas, sounds, sights, and gardens that I found hidden throughout Israel's countryside.

Unfortunately, visiting Rosh Pina was still very much an escape from Tel Aviv, the other fearful side of my personal mountain. This cornerstone—as much as I loved it—was not in the right place. It simply did not fit in Tel Aviv.

Nahal Hazor

CHAPTER SIX

Blue

Seeking Refuge Nearby

Because I was not yet prepared to deal with Tel Aviv, my escape from the city was always imminent. Fleeing to Rosh Pina, however, demanded a serious amount of time; therefore, I found a place to escape to just north of Tel Aviv, about a fifteen-minute drive from our apartment. Blue, a weather-beaten wooden restaurant with glass walls on the sand that looked out on an empty expanse of beach, became my solace. I had a cappuccino on my first visit. Filling my lungs with sea air, I watched people walk in slowly after hectic days to unwind and enjoy the darkening sky. Lifting their aperitifs, they would sigh as the sound of the crash-ing waves swept away their stress. Refugees from the crowded cities, they came to Blue to escape. So did I.

I, too, was a refugee—from Miami, from Tel Aviv, even from my own office at home. Inundated by pictures, journals, and documents, I often felt harried and stressed. Even the pressure of a cursor, blinking on the computer in my cluttered office, overwhelmed me.

My visits to Blue were always the same, but satisfying: I would eat, savor, and then pull out my steno notebooks, losing myself in writing.

Roman aqueduct, Caesarea, Israel

In Miami, apartments, homes, stores, and cafés are large. But rooms in Tel Aviv are tiny. Real estate comes at a premium, and I was having trouble adjusting. Feeling claustrophobic, I would throw on a bathing suit under my jeans and let my inner gypsy surge toward the open sea . . . and return to Blue. I watched as children called out to one other beneath the clear blue sky, throwing beach balls back and forth while their mothers and fathers oiled themselves in the baking sun. After sunning myself on the beach, I would order denise grilled with rosemary and fennel, feeling fortunate to live in a Mediterranean country where there is an abundance of fresh fish.

Blue, outside Tel Aviv

I developed a habit of arriving before noon to have Blue's standard breakfast of softly scrambled eggs with roughly mashed avocado and chunks of onion, slices of fragrant tomatoes, homemade strawberry jam in season, dark muffins with chopped nuts, cream cheese, and slabs of salty Bulgarian goat cheese.

Accompanying the meal was a woven straw basket that contained three toasted rolls lightly dotted with coarse salt and *ketsach*—nigella or Roman coriander—a small black seed with a familiar taste. Though not a light breakfast, it was Blue's standard and, I rationalized, refugees must indulge when they can. If I arrived after noon, I had a choice of many entrées, but I preferred the foie gras in Calvados and seafood salad with calamari and shrimp.

In the winter, when the sea crashed over the stone jetty in cascades of white foam and the dark sky was filled with thunderclouds whipped by the wind, Blue would be practically empty, and that's how I liked it best. Smelling the hickory smoke from the chimney—where I knew a fire was burning in the corner metal stove—I would make my way down the wooden slatted walkway. Clutching my padded jacket close around my neck, my hair flew in every direction until I reached the restaurant on the isolated beach. Once inside, I always took the table near the toasty stove, even though my clothes reeked from hickory smoke when I left. The waiters, dressed in white shirts and black trousers covered by a long, royal blue apron, awaited me. Cozy and protected against the elements that beat furiously against the glass walls, I would often—and still do—sit for hours, reading a book or writing and sipping coffee.

To be protected on a stormy day evokes the most profound sense of refuge. Over the years, I've come to Blue at different times of the day and at various seasons. It is not elegant; I do not know the proprietor or even his name. But as in a good friendship, I've grown to trust it. It won't let me down. And I enjoy all its moods. I've shared Blue with Ted and almost no one else.

Dor Habonim coast, Israel

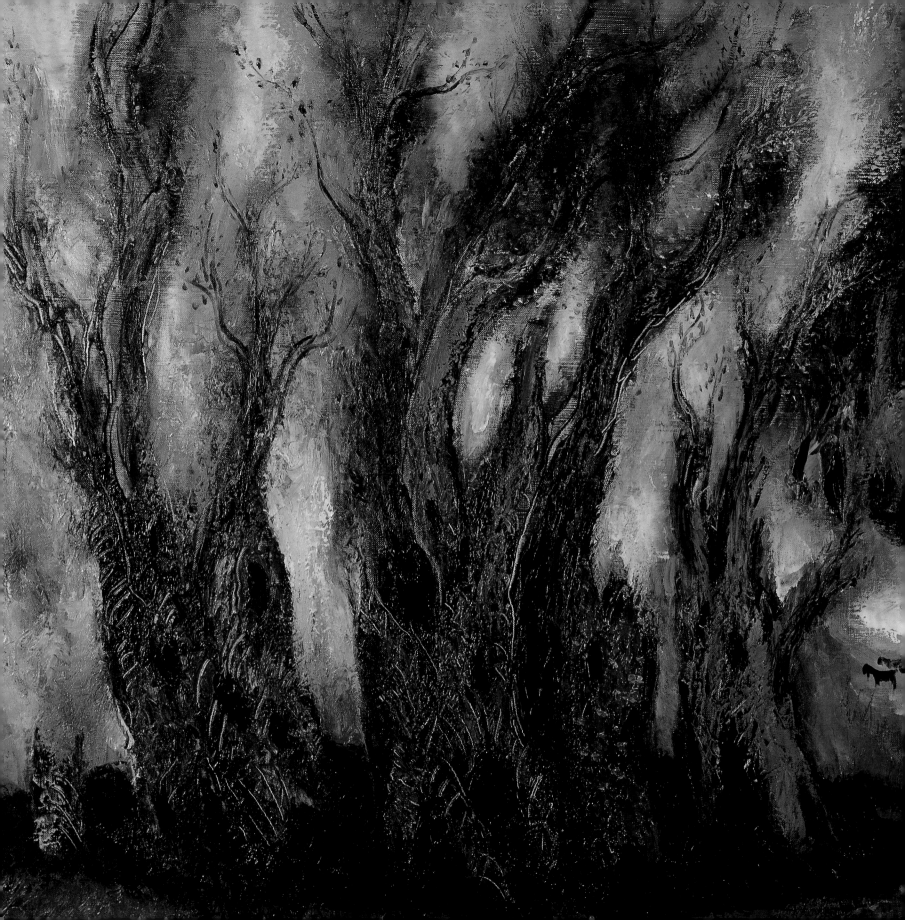

CHAPTER SEVEN

Painted Olives

Entering the Picture

When Ted and I were married in Miami, he brought with him an Israeli painting of an olive grove. The painting unnerved me. Massive tree trunks with their dark, ominous caverns appeared to be twisted into a macabre dance, their limbs uplifted and swaying in the swirling mist. A few goats and a cloaked rider on a donkey passed between the trees, while two barefoot women in blue robes followed a few paces behind. The scene evoked mystery and foreign lands; and though it was part of Ted's past, it disturbed me. The painting hung on the walls of our many apartments— first in Miami, then Monaco—until it finally came back home when we moved to Israel.

Reuven Rubin painted the mysterious olive trees in the early 1900s, and it was only after I met his widow, Esther, that the painting finally became less daunting. I first met Esther at her home on Bialik Street in Tel Aviv, where she and her late husband had lived and raised their two children. I was scouting for material for my column in *Link* magazine, writing about the Rubins' home,

Once the painting had seemed foreign and threatening, but after Esther and I became friends, I was able to see it with new eyes.

Olive grove painting by Reuven Rubin

which Esther had turned into an intimate museum after her husband's death in 1974. Still hovering over it as she had when Rubin was alive, she seemed at home in her Tel Aviv museum. She also seemed very American. Her very large, light green eyes radiated intelligence and warmth, and my interviews with her developed into a deep friendship. Esther soon became both a role model and a kindred spirit.

She'd led a fascinating life. As a seventeen-year-old New Yorker, Esther Davis won an oratory contest where first prize was a round-trip transatlantic cruise. It proved to be a one-way journey. On the *Mauritania* heading from New York to Israel, she met the thirty-six-year-old Rubin, who proposed within minutes of seeing her on deck. As he wrote later in his autobiography, Rubin was immediately captivated by her sea-green eyes—they struck him as sensuously strong and deep. Artists and most women rely on their instincts to make decisions, and Rubin knew at once that Esther was the right woman for him. They

Reuven Rubin's painting of Esther

were married within the year.

Young Esther gave Rubin new life. She joined him in Israel and soon became his protector, answering the phones, writing letters, and arranging for financial support of his exhibitions so that he could concentrate on painting. Esther was a strong woman, but in our interviews she always made certain I didn't overestimate her contribution to her husband's work. She had only facilitated and supported him. Rubin, she reminded me, was a self-made man; before that fateful shipboard meeting, he had even been given an exhibition by Alfred Steiglitz in New York. But it was equally obvious to me that her presence had deeply affected his work.

Esther showed me around the museum. Their former Tel Aviv home was devoid of furniture except for Rubin's studio on the third floor. Its oversized wooden table, covered with partially used tubes of paint and paintbrushes stuffed into earthenware mugs, stood against the far wall next to a woven rattan lounge. The scene clearly suggested that Rubin might return at any

The Rubins' love story reminded me of my own. Ted claimed that he, too, was immediately captivated—by my smile, strength, and independence. Like Rubin, he also made an astonishingly quick decision about whether we were meant for each other. Still, it took us two years before we were married.

Olive trees in Dir Hanna, Israel

Esther and I had a lot in common. Like me, Esther had assumed much control over her life with her husband, but ironically, she also had to surrender part of herself. Wistfully, she sometimes wonders about the road not taken, the career she might have had. But despite her occasional feelings of uncertainty, she feels no regret. She sacrificed for her husband out of love. So did I.

Reuven Rubin's painting of himself and Esther

moment, pick up his brushes, coil his lanky body onto a stool, lean toward the easel, and finish the canvas of the two fishermen throwing their nets.

Indeed, tours of schoolchildren loved seeing where the artist worked—and so did I. Lacking a well-developed concept of time, children could sense that the studio was alive with Rubin's presence. Esther reveled in that presence, too. She needed to retain and perpetuate her husband—that part of her

Olive tree in Dir Hanna

windows, I saw the beginnings of Tel Aviv: Among the sand dunes were a few square houses and many tents, while sailboats scudded along the blue sea in the distance. A brick minaret pierced the cobalt sky, while large steamships and sailboats waited patiently in the port of Jaffa to load their cargoes. Now the port of Jaffa no longer caters to cargo and is filled with fishing vessels selling their daily catch on the dock. But some things have not

younger self that was created by him. She did so by allowing a part of her life to still revolve around the museum. For Esther, it was a way of both maintaining and letting go.

Every wall of the Rubin Museum was filled with his paintings. On the ground floor was a self-portrait of young Rubin as a pioneer, wearing a white open-necked shirt and holding a single flower coaxed from the barren land of Palestine. In the old family living room, a larger painting depicted a bronze, shirtless pioneer, his powerful hands steadying a ripe watermelon on his muscular shoulders. Next to him, a kneeling woman cradled a luscious orange miraculously harvested from the arid land.

In another painting, through Rubin's painted

changed: The sycamore trees shown in the painting still flourish on King George Street, thanks to Rubin's benevolence. They were to be razed when the street was built, but Rubin persuaded the city to save six of them in the median strip. Later, when walking along King George Street, I found comfort in these massive, voluptuous trees. They seemed to affirm his existence, as did his studio in the Rubin Museum.

The museum's front room displayed a portrait of a young, affianced Rubin and Esther, sitting on a wrought-iron terrace in the sunlight, she with her startling green eyes and he with his red slippers, announcing to the world that he felt at home in Israel. And, of course, there were several paintings of his renowned olive trees. These particularly attracted my

attention, partly because I knew why he had come to paint the landscape with such passion: His marriage to Esther had changed his art. Rubin revealed this in his autobiography. . . .

Life with Esther gave me a new, optimistic attitude, which I had never known before. Suddenly, the landscape and flowers became living reality . . . I can recall exactly when this happened . . . I was on my way to Jerusalem with Esther on one of our many trips together. We approached the beautiful village of Abu Ghosh, surrounded by ancient olive trees. I stopped the car and stood amazed, for I saw the countryside in a completely different way than I ever

Olive grove near Makkabim

had before. It seemed to me that the landscape and its olive trees were leaning toward me, embracing me. The colors, the light, the shimmering atmosphere in which the landscape seemed to breathe and live . . . it was like a revelation.

Rubin might have been talking about the olive trees in our painting that lean forward, giving the illusion that they are wrapping their limbs around the viewer. Suddenly it became warm and familiar, as if the two

women portrayed were Esther and myself, following the man in the picture deep into Israel's olive tree forest.

I was beginning to understand Rubin's experience with the olive tree. Surprisingly, the tree had reached out to me, too, when I first moved to Israel. On the terrace of our first apartment in a small neighborhood called Bavli, in northern Tel Aviv, there was a planter with space for a tree. Instinctively, I knew it had to be an olive tree. Over the next few years, I'd monitored its slow, sturdy growth. Its silvery leaves regally presided over pink geraniums and fuchsia cyclamens; then a year later it began to offer fruit, which stained the beige slate tiles of the terrace with splatters of deep purple. I had lived in Mediterranean lands where the olive tree is a common and reassuring sight, but until moving to Israel I had never lived in such close proximity to one. With growing awareness, I absorbed its subtle development and cycles.

Four years later we switched apartments, but I chose to leave my olive tree behind. I didn't want to disturb its precise, careful growth by uprooting it. Somehow, through my relationship with Esther, I'd discovered a sensitivity for the olive tree. I didn't need to take it with me. It was enough that I was being uprooted again.

Ancient olive trees in Dir Hanna

Olive trees, Galilee

CHAPTER EIGHT

Real Olives

Taking Root

I did not plant an olive tree on the terrace of our new apartment. Again, I found my salvation on the open road—by driving out into the countryside to find olive trees planted hundreds of years ago. They were easy to discover. I was now living in a Mediterranean land, and olive trees flourished here. The trees reminded me of the ones Ted and I had seen when traveling in Mallorca, Greece, Italy, and France. There were groves of them, just like in our painting, just like I found wherever I explored Israel. Without my knowing it, they became a part of me.

This happened in an unexpected way. . . . I was researching a Galilee olive oil festival for a magazine article when I discovered Shaul Eger on his farm in Yokne'am. Shaul's olive oil is sold in specialty stores all over Israel and reputed to be among the very best in the country. I wanted to learn about the growing of olives and the pressing of oil, and I thought Shaul's farm would be a good place to start.

I sat with Shaul and his wife, Rina, in their

Olive trees inhabit a part of the world where time passes slowly and aging is an art. The Mediterranean has a stately pace that ennobles both the fruit and those who nurture it.

Ancient olive press

living room, eating delicious green olives. We talked about olives, and soon the subject led into history. More than just a haven for growing olives, Shaul's town possessed a rich past. Shaul told me that at the nearby crossroads there was a tel, a hill of earth, covering the remains of the old town of Yokne'am on the ancient Via Maris, a sea road lined with olive groves. Fascinated, I visualized the travelers coming from Mesopotamia toward the Mediterranean Sea. When my historical questions became too detailed, Shaul suggested I seek out David Eitam, an archaeologist who had also been the curator and director of the Israel Oil Industry Museum in Haifa and still had access to the archives. Meeting with David would quench my curiosity about both history and olives.

I met with David soon after, and he informed me that in ancient Israel, olive pressing and cultivation had started around 9000 to 6000 B.C., but that wild olive trees had been growing throughout the Mediterranean for some forty-five thousand years. I wasn't surprised. No wonder they seemed to be such an integral part of the landscape!

David first brought me to a modern—and sanitized—olive press in the Galilee. It looked like any other factory: very efficient and not very charming. But, as I would later discover, the charm of traditional presses—such as the one in nearby Yanuch—was offset

David Eitam

by an age-old layer of grime. David explained to me that the older presses spout out mashed olives, which are then spread on woven burlap mats in layers. Those are squeezed until the oil-and-water mixture is subsequently separated by centrifugal force. Then the oil settles for three months before it can be sold.

The process was less efficient, but still in distinct contrast to a time when humans and animals had toiled at even more ancient traditional olive presses. At the Land of Israel Museum in Tel Aviv, I'd seen on display a large upright grinding stone turned by a donkey. But at David's Israel Oil Industry Museum was the oldest press of all: a small bowl carved into limestone, in

Shaul began growing olive trees for his health: He had discovered that fifty milliliters of olive oil in his food every day cured his heart condition. I stored this information in the back of my mind, determined to investigate the health benefits of olive oil. Ted had recently been ill, and I wondered if it might be good for him, too.

which the olives were beaten with a hand-held grinding stone. Water was added to the mixture, and the oil floated to the top. Then the fresh olive oil exited the bowl through a shallow stone trough and dripped down into a stone receptacle below.

After we'd seen the presses, David elaborated on the history of olive oil in ancient Israel. He took me to a park in the Galilee called Rosh Zeit, and there, amidst the stone ruins of the village of Kabul, the past came alive. According to David, King Solomon presented Kabul, a town rich in olive oil, to the king of Tyre in exchange for the cedars of Lebanon, which were used to build Israel's First Temple.

David drew imaginary castles in the air. "Here are their houses," he gestured, referring to the town, "and there are the oil presses and rooms filled with large pottery amphorae to store the oil."

We then turned from his imaginary descriptions to see the remains of a wooden lever, weights that fit into a stone used for the pressing, and limestone remnants lying in the fresh, thick grass dotted with red anemones all dappled in the spring sun. He even showed me shards of Israeli oil amphorae, dated from 4000 B.C. Discovered in Greece, these shards present

Olives, Carmel Market, Tel Aviv

evidence that olive oil was exported from Israel much earlier than had previously been thought. Because Israel did not have abundant forests, the olive oil presses were cut in stone from the hewn limestone found in the hills of the Galilee. Many remains still exist.

I spent several days exploring with David. Later, he challenged me to learn the differences in the taste of oils. I expected something akin to cod liver oil, which I had been forced to swallow as a child. Sipping from a wineglass, I found the texture of olive oil a pleasant surprise. I dipped my nose into the glass and breathed in the heavy scent. It reminded me of Greek salads served on sunny island coasts. Sipping, I rolled the oil inside my mouth, allowing its full flavor to register. A few oils had a cloying, sweet taste, as if the olives had been ripening too long and were now turning moldy. Indeed, this was the case—these oils were becoming rancid. Some of the oils also had a biting aftertaste, which I learned was caused by bruised fruit, unclean presses, or sitting in the burlap sacks too long.

Between tastes, I sampled apple slices to clear my palate. My favorite oil turned out to be a freshly pressed Souri, which had the flavor of sweet, fresh

Rosh Zayit in the ancient village of Kabul, Israel

meadows. Some of the Israeli olive oil had become more sophisticated than what I had known. A few olive oil makers like David have achieved the standards of the extra-virgin oil of Italy and France.

I was then handed a withered black olive flaked with coarse white salt. David had placed ripe black olives under a light stone in a wooden tray to be slowly pressed for several months. I brushed off the salt and chewed slowly as heavy olive oil coated my lips. The delicious flavor enveloped me—it was heady and pungent.

The time I spent with David, learning about olive oil, influenced me the same way my relationship with Esther Rubin had: As I became more acquainted with the people of Mediterranean Israel and the venerable olive tree, I was more drawn to it. Much later in the Galilee, I encountered an ancient olive tree. It must have been at least a thousand years old. It was not the familiar olive tree of Rubin's painting but a real one with an immense, thickly gnarled trunk and cavernous black hollows. I smelled the earth entwined in its shallow roots. This was not one of the olive trees that I had admired while

Olive press at Eretz Israel Museum

on vacation in Mallorca or France or Italy. This was a real olive tree in Israel—my home.

"I'm not just passing through," I told myself quietly. "I live here."

I reached out to steady myself against its massive trunk, my fingers touching the inside of the hollows where part of the tree had died. Suddenly no longer threatening, it felt ragged and flaking with age. Young shoots of sinewy lifelines had grown around the caverns to compensate for sickness, death, and disintegration. I sank down into the grass at the base of the old olive tree, wondering how many years it had taken to form the fierce, gnarled foundation that could survive so many changes and the harsh, inclement climate of the land. This particular old olive tree had witnessed many civilizations, yet I knew that each year its sinuous limbs had sprouted fresh young leaves and succulent, robust fruit.

I lay on the grass under my worn and weathered tree. Even though I had become an independent traveler in Israel, I finally felt I shared Ted's roots. His dowry of olive trees had become mine—a mutual legacy.

*I could not escape the enormous presence of this olive tree,
so much more powerful than the macabre dance that seemed to reach
out to me from the painting so many years ago.*

Olive tree on the Golan

CHAPTER NINE

Zichron Yaacov

Roots for the Rootless

Years ago on one of our annual visits to Israel, Ted took me to Zichron Yaacov, a small village an hour north of Tel Aviv, where his family had first settled. Up the hill from the Carmel Winery were the remains of what had been his Grandfather Moshe's barn. The wood was weather-beaten and disheveled after one hundred years of wear. Large patches of blue sky showed through the rafters, but the metal horseshoes on the door were intact.

Then Ted brought me to the cemetery where his family was buried. Reluctantly, I followed him, remembering his mother's funeral in Tel Aviv. I had been shocked to see the outline of her body under a white sheet as it slid into a deep hole in the red earth. I had not been aware of the burial customs in Israel, as stark and real as the cycles of nature. There are no coffins, nothing to disguise death. As we searched among the headstones in Zichron, a wizened old man wearing a blue beret appeared out of nowhere. We introduced ourselves, and when he heard Ted's family name, the man was awestruck. He motioned for

I was becoming more and more drawn to this tiny country. Inspired by the renewal at Zichron, I drove from one end of Israel to the other, taking it into my possession and then sharing it through my writing.

Nahal Alon, Carmel

us to follow him across the street, where Ted's great-grandparents' and grandparents' names were inscribed on a wall of rose-colored clay along with the other founders who had sailed from Romania and arrived in Zichron, then called Zammarin, in 1882.

Next to the founders' wall was a small commemorative room, where—incredibly—pictures of Ted's great-grandparents, his grandparents, and even his parents were displayed. Groups of somber people standing near a ship and dressed in old-fashioned clothes stared at us from the faded photographs. Ted was overcome. He knew his relatives had been among the first settlers, but he remembered them as hard-working and humble—not particularly heroic. He was surprised that such a monument had been erected in this tiny village, where he had so many fond childhood memories, such as the smell of bread baking in a taboon of clay fueled by cow dung, family feasts at holidays, and picking almonds in the summertime for his grandfather.

I, however, had no childhood memories of Zichron Yaacov; to me the town seemed dark and unappealing. Derelict farmhouses stood bereft and untended on the original street, which ran across the ridge of the mountain. There were no restaurants or boutiques—nothing interesting to poke around in. The whole town seemed devoid of charm.

Ted and I left the pioneers in the commemorative room and made our way to Arie and Leah Arison's farm, nestled among the orange groves in the neighboring town of Binyamina, beneath the cliffs of Zichron. I was looking forward to Aunt Leah's turkey and chicken schnitzel followed by her fabulous chocolate-covered almond and hazelnut cake. The good food and company always delighted me during our visits to the old homestead.

As we pulled up, we watched Uncle Arie at work on his tractor, peacefully tending to his crops. Immediately, I envisioned his father Moshe in his horse-drawn wagon, bound for his Zichron vineyards. There is something timeless about the land and growing crops. Although I have never lived on a farm, I imagine most small farms closely resemble their predecessors. Seeing Arie and Leah's took me back in time.

After Uncle Arie passed away and Aunt Leah moved to a nursing home, we rarely returned to Zichron. One day, however, Ted's sister informed me that a fine chef had renovated one of the old, crumbling

When Ted planted a vegetable garden in our yard in Miami, it remained a mystery to me; I was startled to see green vines clustered with round red tomatoes. As a New Yorker, my experience with food had been restricted to the supermarket, where tomatoes were set out in gray cardboard trays covered with Saran wrap. But after visiting Zichron, I understood why Ted needed to grow vegetables—it was a part of his heritage.

Beit Daniel in Zichron Yaacov

farmhouses in a courtyard on Pioneer Street. Intrigued, I drove the hour north to try the cuisine. To my pleasant surprise, I discovered that some of the other farmers' courtyards had already been renovated into pubs, restaurants, and quaint boutiques. Stone fountains, umbrellas shading alfresco dining, terracotta rooftops, geraniums, a proliferation of multihued bougainvillea, mulberry trees for making paper instead of feeding silkworms, jars of

Zichron Yaacov

homemade marmalade, cheeses, honey, and olive oil conjured up the French countryside. Zichron had certainly changed since our visits—much for the better.

I found the restaurant, Picciotto's, midway up the main street next to a stone wall lined with hanging baskets that held bright red geraniums. Gil de Picciotto, the owner, had covered the farmhouse with burnt siena stucco, leaving one corner untouched to show the original worn stones. A fighter pilot in the reserves one day a week, Gil is also an exemplary chef. Although he claims the French- and Italian-style cheeses made in

Israel are catching on, his own fare does not call for the use of heavy cheese. For his roasted beet and vegetable terrine he still uses the traditional light goat cheese that he gets from the Berkowitzes' farm across the street, where Mr. Berkowitz raises the goats and Mrs. Berkowitz makes the cheese.

Gil approaches his cooking as an art, with the kind of precision one might expect from a fighter pilot after dark. He lightly braises fish so as not to destroy the texture and uses a butter-based emulsion to bring out the flavor, combining rosemary with quail, red wine with beef, and regularly including Israel's foie gras. Gil chooses sauces that enhance the taste of his dishes. His menu is Mediterranean, but he has his own ideas about what to use and how to mix different elements together. He uses the new Israeli olive oil, elegant and refined, as well as the more earthy, robust variety in his cooking.

He and his friend Ronen Raviv, who also has a delightful restaurant, Il Bacio, just a few doors away,

As a fighter pilot, Gil must defend the land like the pioneers who returned to Israel once did. Since all babies born in Israel eventually must become soldiers—first in active service, then in the reserves—they live split lives. They are soldiers at the same time they are computer salespeople, sound engineers, doctors, and chefs. As all Israeli soldiers must, Gil learned to balance the extremes of his life, defending his country while also experimenting with sauces, and blending tastes and aromas. His heroism in the cockpit adds an unexpected dimension to the elegance and softness he displays in his kitchen.

פיצ'וטו

PICCIOTTO

פיצ'
יוTTO

דג
חנות →

משפחה

Gil Picciotto at his restaurant in Zichron Yaacov

even make their own wine. The Israeli palate is changing in regard to wine, Gil claims. Most Israelis used to drink the semi-dry whites, but eighty percent have now switched to red. Gil has had ample opportunity to test that theory: On Fridays, Picciotto's traditionally has wine tastings, attracting a group of connoisseurs who banter good-naturedly with each other—much like the atmosphere of a Parisian café.

Beit Daniel, Zichron Yaacov

Lunch at Picciotto's was delicious, just as my sister-in-law had promised. I ate on the terrace, overlooking the cobblestoned Pioneer Street, savoring each bite. The experience reminded me of South Beach's rebirth, and the first renovation of a Miami Art Deco hotel. . . .

I had rushed to the old Carlyle Hotel with an artist friend for an upscale meal served on the terrace overlooking Ocean Avenue. We soaked in the sun and admired the sand and vibrant blue sky, ignoring the decay all around us. When my friend smelled the salt air and pined for a studio in the otherwise desolate beach town, I knew that South Beach would come back to life.

Ted and I later participated in the renaissance by buying an abandoned movie theater on Lincoln Road Mall and converting it into a small concert hall and

offices for the New World Symphony. I still reminisce with our Miami friends about that time, recalling our enthusiastic jaunts through the dismal streets of South Beach, when we noted even the smallest changes with delight. Eventually, the renewal developed momentum, and now "SoBe" houses artists' studios, boutiques, and interesting restaurants.

Like South Beach's renewal, Zichron's restoration proceeded rapidly—so much so that I often drove there with friends to note the progress. But in spite of the splendid views of the Mediterranean from Zichron's large modern hotels and new villas perched on the cliffs, my favorite haunts remained farther inland in the old village on the hilltop. I often walked along the dirt paths of Beit Daniel, a handsome estate turned music center, listening to musicians practice for their evening concerts. During festivals, the doors of a small wooden theater were thrown open to music lovers, who sat on a grassy knoll under the stars, listening to chamber music in the fresh pine-scented air.

I also explored less popular sites. Near the communal dining room, at the end of a deserted driveway

Once I'd learned about the family's involvement in Zichron, I, too, wanted to give back to the land. So in Grandfather Moshe's tradition, I invested in a marketing company for Israeli wines. I love to see grapes, lush and heavy on the vines, crushed and fermented under the artistic hand of the winemaker.

lined with towering royal palms and ancient cypress trees, stood another treasured haunt: the stone ruins of the historical Lange House. The decaying, oriental-style mansion had gripped me at once: I recognized it as the mysterious ruin I'd read about many years before in Amos Oz's novel *Black Box*. It possessed and enchanted me—it was a place that had seemingly come alive from the pages of such a moving narrative.

Over time, I also became interested in the continuing history of Lange House and its legacy of art: Muriel Bentwich's gentle watercolors. Muriel had lived with her sister Nita and brother-in-law Michael Lange, who built the compound in 1912 and called it Carmel Court. There, Muriel was inspired to paint. Her paintings reveal her deep affection for Israel, and her delicate palette perfectly captures the beauty of Zichron—Mediterranean simplicity at its best.

I was not the only one in our family who had found Zichron so promising. Soon after I rediscovered it, Ted's daughter, Shari, did as well. Because of her family's role in the town's history, she was approached to renovate Zichron's Old Council Building into a museum that told the story of the first pioneers. Intrigued, she agreed to take on the project. Part of the process included publishing a book about the pioneers, and through that Shari learned more about her great-grandfather. She discovered, to her delight, that she and Moshe shared several traits: a propensity for neatness, punctuality, and tenacity.

Moshe kept his tools sharpened and neatly arranged; Shari's precise desk is very much the same. Only eleven when he accompanied his older sister and brother-in-law to Israel, Moshe's determination and attention to detail paid off: Eventually he became a successful farmer who could coax robust purple grapes out of the arid, rocky land.

Shari was also surprised to learn that our relatives had been involved in local winemaking. The family vineyard was located near the Carmel Winery, Baron Edmond de Rothschild's large, commercial facility, which had cool and damp French-style cellars to age the wine. In a cooperative venture, the Arisons sold their grapes to the Rothschilds, helping to establish modern Israel's wine industry.

Shari's years of carefully building the museum enriched her significantly—and me as well, for it better acquainted me with my husband's family. Since I'd never had the opportunity to meet Ted's father, Meir, who died when Ted was young, visiting Zichron provided some compensation for me. There, I heard many stories about his father, some that reminded me of Ted. For example, at his bar mitzvah, Meir had received a cow from the village so he could start his own farm. But he wanted to be a businessman, not a farmer. So he sold the cow and used the money to finance a voyage to Costa, the largest city in Turkey—now called Istanbul—in order to continue his education.

Mount Tabor from Nahal Tabor

Another tale described how Ted's father, drafted as an officer in the Turkish army in World War I, was transferred to Zichron, where he boldly bribed a fellow Turkish officer to free one of the settlers from captivity and torturous interrogation. The settler was a member of Nili, a spy ring formed to help the British expel the Turks from Palestine. The conspirators agreed to supply the British forces in Egypt with military secrets in exchange for arms to be used for the future liberation of the country. Clandestine meetings were held at Nili's headquarters in the Aaronson house on Pioneer Street. Now a museum, it contains the Aaronson family's furniture and shows where young Sara Aaronson hid the rifle she used to commit suicide to avoid further torture by the Turks after she had surrendered to protect the rest of the family.

My experiences in Zichron allowed me to explore Ted's rich heritage, and as a result enriched my marriage. In characteristic fashion, Ted had initially downplayed his family's contribution to the small village. But once he saw the public's overwhelmingly positive response to the museum, he became less reticent and began to identify with his powerful family roots. His father had turned his back on farming to enter business, and Ted had followed in those footsteps. Both of them had returned to Israel under heroic and unusual circumstances.

Zichron indeed had transformed itself from a state of disrepair and neglect into a charming town. For me, Zichron will always be much more than a beautiful Mediterranean village. The family stories rooted here have become deeply personal—a mix of history, personalities, and even outright heroism.

CHAPTER TEN

Wine and Cheese
With Harry

*M*y brother Harry was coming to Israel for a few days, and I felt compelled to share with him the treasures I had recently discovered. Harry is five years younger than I, and when we were growing up, I thought I was supposed to pass on valuable information to him. I still have this inclination to educate him, which he suffers graciously and, occasionally, gratefully.

Several years ago, we'd revisited our old New York neighborhood, Washington Heights. As we reminisced, Harry told me he had not ventured out onto the black metal fire escape outside our apartment to catch the summer breeze because there was not enough room for both of us. I was touched by his kindness. We then walked to the park across the street, where we learned something else about each other: There we had shared the same milky quartz fault that ran through a dark granite boulder. It had served as my throne when I'd played princess, and I was astonished to find out that Harry had used the same rock as his horse when, as a

Harry enjoyed being with the artists of the land— bringing forth a better wine . . . a better cheese— and he was happy to be there at its inception.

Abbey of Latrun, Israel

cowboy, he'd ridden off into the Upper Manhattan sunset. We had never before confided that we'd played make-believe—and I was delighted to find out that my very logical brother also had a dream world when he was young.

Our time together in New York, visiting our childhood haunts, had drawn us even closer. Now in Israel, I was eager to show Harry around my new neighborhood. After a casual morning spent strolling through Tel Aviv,

Shaul Elkana, owner, Gaffen Wine Shop

we headed out of town. I drove him into the hills of Jerusalem to Eli Ben Zaken's winery, where the smell of fermenting grapes brought back memories of the bouquets of wine we had inhaled in the south of France and Italy.

I had discovered Eli Ben Zaken's Castel winery years ago by happenstance.

⌣

I was exploring the German Colony in Jerusalem, enjoying the narrow, intimate lanes and high stone walls covered with flowers. It reminded me of the outskirts of Saint-Tropez, where Ted and I had walked through the vineyards in the cool mornings on our way to the beach. I looked into the Gaffen Wine Shop on Emek Refaim Street to check their stock and met Shaul

Elkana. Shaul was easygoing and informative, and I found myself consulting him and readily absorbing his knowledge of Israeli wines. He mentioned Eli Ben Zaken, who had been touted by the master of wine at Sotheby. Interested, I phoned Eli, and he gave me directions to Ramat Razi'el, where he lived.

Driving the hairpin turns up the pine-covered mountains, with only a metal railing separating me from the sheer drops into the valleys near Bet Shemesh, I felt as if I were in Switzerland. When I arrived at Eli's house, I was taken by the simple beauty of the countryside: The garden overlooked a deep chasm bordered by mountains shadowed in sunset. Eli and his wife, Monique, came out of their Provençal home to greet me. We sat at their marble-topped picnic table and tasted his 1993 Grand Vin Castel. From a tree in his garden, Eli picked a pod off a limb, cracked it open, and handed me two sweet halves of a walnut to eat.

⌣

With vivid memories of my first trip to the winery, I arrived with Harry at Eli Ben Zaken's. Painted an earthy pumpkin color with sky blue trim, the Tuscan and Provençal hues, Ben Zaken's winery—or

The Ben Zaken home

"temple," as he called it—was located at the foot of the mountain vineyard he had planted on the hillside just below his home.

After greeting the Ben Zakens, I led Harry down the narrow staircase to the cool cellars. In typical Bordeaux fashion, Ben Zaken had painted the casks dusky rose to mask the wine that drips when the winemaker tastes the vintage. We then went to the vineyards, where he had banded his vines to wire supports in equidistant rows, and had counted and pruned each bunch of grapes exactly according to formula.

We marveled at Ben Zaken's attention to detail and aesthetics; it was, we knew, the reason for the aristocratic taste of his Castel wine. In 1992, Sotheby's wine expert had praised Ben Zaken's first vintage of six hundred bottles as the best wine in Israel; each year thereafter, the auction house had been similarly effusive. In addition to his prize-winning red wine—from a combination of Cabernet Sauvignon and Merlot grapes—Ben Zaken told us he would soon be making a Chardonnay. No longer a tiny family venture, the winery planned to produce 100,000 bottles by 2003. As we left the winery to have lunch at a rustic restaurant hidden near the

Eli Ben Zaken, owner and winemaker, Castel wine

top of the mountain, I took along two bottles of the new vintage of Grand Vin Castel.

Harry was pleasantly surprised at the terra-cotta-roofed houses and the fresh air that permeated the Judean hills. Sitting on the wooden planked terrace in Ramat Razi'el, he breathed in deeply, relishing the view of the gorge beneath us. The gorge was typical of the Jerusalem hills—sparsely vegetated, mostly mottled by stones—and Harry, a nature lover like me, was drawn to it.

I had found the restaurant some years ago while exploring a road near the winery. Not only did it provide fine French cuisine, it also served as an art gallery. On the menu seared foie gras was offered with four sauces: raspberry, fig, honey, and mustard. As a dutiful older sister, I ordered myself a serving with fig just so my brother could taste it. He was too disciplined to order something so fattening, but he was glad to sample mine.

After we finished dining, we made our way higher up the mountains to the Sattaf, a national park where Shai Zeltzer's goat farm was located. Several years ago, Ben Zaken had brought me to his friend Shai, and I had been grateful to be introduced. Now I was

The Ben Zaken home

eager for him to meet Harry. After a difficult drive on a winding dirt road, following the rough, gray wooden signs marked with a painted goat, we arrived at the farm.

Cradling the two bottles of Castel wine in our arms, Harry and I carefully made our way past the wooden pens of brown and white goats to the ancient stone cave where one of Shai's children was weighing and selling the cheeses that Shai had made in his dairy. Giving her one of the bottles of wine, I asked her to deliver it to Shai by way of announcing our arrival. She quickly returned, leading us to a platform in the sky above the cave, where we looked out in every direction. Just below us was the tin roof of a small, white-tiled building—the dairy where Shai made his cheese—and to the left were the goat pens. A green valley, threaded by a winding road, flanked another mountain, which lay in front of us.

Shai glided gracefully down the steps chiseled into the hillside above, leading from the home he had built. Wearing a loose white cotton shirt, his trousers tied at his waist, he was a peaceful sight. His white beard was flowing and his hair was caught in a rubber band at the nape of his neck. Waving to us, his

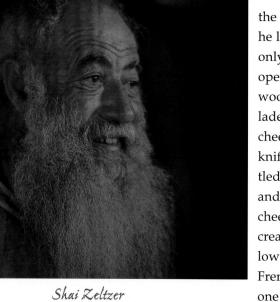
Shai Zeltzer

light blue eyes shone warmly with welcome.

When I offered Shai the second bottle of wine, he left us for a moment only to return with an opener, wineglasses, a wooden cutting board laden with tall wedges of cheese, and a serrated knife. Then everyone settled back to drinking wine and tasting cheese. The cheese was delicious: The creamy one with the yellow rind was like the French Tomme; a sharper one tasted like a German Muenster; and another one with a nutty flavor—thick with green veins and a moldy gray-brown rind— tasted like a superb Italian Gorgonzola.

Years ago, Shai regularly gave away a third of his production for tasting in order to teach people about cheese. Often they would make a face, sputtering, "Ooh, the smell." I understood this only too well: When I was growing up, the smell of strong cheeses also made me gag. I barely tolerated the tasteless Velveeta and bland slices of American cheese wrapped in cellophane. Aged cheese is an acquired taste. But now, thanks in part to Shai, many Israelis, including myself, have successfully made this culinary transition.

Machines can separate the curds from the whey, but Shai enjoys the feel of the cheese in his hands as it turns from a slightly jelled texture into a spongy mass. It seems a miracle to him each time the liquid turns into a solid without curdling; until he is sure of success, he always holds his breath.

Shai impressed my brother as a gifted intellectual, and I knew Harry was charmed by him. Harry had done a lot of traveling himself, and he looked perfectly comfortable in this wild setting.

"How did you come to this mountain?" he asked our host.

Shai told us he had been an instructor of botany at Hebrew University, but after serving in the Yom Kippur War, he could not bring himself to return to academe. What he'd seen as a soldier had changed him forever. So for three years he worked with the government to help a few aimless teenagers become more emotionally stable, working with them at a nearby farm until they were ready to join the army. Shai was no longer at a formal university, but he was still teaching. After the teenagers left, he began to raise goats. A monk at the abbey down the mountain taught him to make cheese—and Shai discovered his calling.

For years, Shai traveled around the world to learn how to make the cheeses native to other countries. He found, for example, that each village in France has diverse plants, trees, and bacteria in the air; as a result, France has some four hundred unique cheeses. Eventually, Shai was able to produce as many as six different cheeses by using various bacteria in each vat of goat's milk.

Years before, I'd asked Shai if I could watch him make the cheese. Being literal-minded, I could not understand how he used bacteria unless I saw it. I visualized test tubes with cork stoppers in a metal rack like in chemistry class. But it wasn't like that at all.

Shai's bacteria came sealed in square flat tinfoil packets of powder printed with neat labels. The night before I came, he had mixed the bacteria into cartons of sterile milk. The next morning, he poured the mixture into vats of heated goat's milk, moving with the grace of an artist. I watched as he stirred the surface of the milk, causing it to ripple just like the pot of junket my mother used to heat slowly over the stove. Junket, a favorite dessert of my childhood, was sweetened, flavored milk set

Inside Shai Zeltzer's cave

Shai marvels at how climate and location affect both cheese and winemaking. The moldy roof of Shai's cave, for instance, contributes to the taste of his cheese. And rainfall and other weather patterns affect the branches and leaves that the goats graze on. One year, a drought gave the cheese a particularly pungent flavor. The same cheese made at sea level tastes completely different.

with rennet. Its powder came in packages that looked like Jell-O Pudding.

Soon the cheese mixture began to solidify. When the consistency was just right, Shai "worked" the cheese. After gently breaking up the junketlike mixture, he slipped on plastic sleeves up to his shoulders and dipped his rubber-gloved hands into the vat in order to separate the curds from the whey. For the first time, I understood what that singsong phrase meant. I sat, fascinated, as Shai feathered his hands through the liquid whey, catching the more solid curds and softly pressing them toward the sides of the tank. He opened a spigot from time to time to siphon off the whey and eventually was left with a spongy mass of curds four inches high at the bottom of the tank. He scooped them up and slapped them into about one hundred translucent plastic molds.

Shai inverted the plastic molds every few minutes until all the liquid drained and the cheese became dense. The following day he removed the cheeses from their containers, salted them, and placed them in his cool, damp cave to age for a year or so.

Sitting on the mountainside with Harry, reminiscing about watching Shai make cheese was relaxing. The air smelled fresh and natural on the mountainside, and so did Shai's dairy. I was not surprised that my brother enjoyed our day together. A businessman, he could see that our two mavericks, Eli Ben Zaken and Shai Zeltzer, would lead the way to changing accepted procedures.

Spending time with me in Israel also helped Harry to adjust to my move. He had always found it difficult to deal with our family's countless relocations. Years before, Harry had asked our parents not to move from New York to Miami, which would leave him to finish college without the physical presence of his family. Parents should be like trees, he informed them, rooted in one place. Unfortunately for Harry, they did move—and eventually so did his big sister. But I'd begun to develop roots in Israel, and Harry found that comforting. Even though we were physically far apart, our experiences in Mediterranean Israel had brought us very close.

Fields, "Burma" Road, Israel

Trees in the Judean hills

CHAPTER ELEVEN

Wine

Distilling the Past

Eli Ben Zaken was not the only pioneer influencing the wine industry of Israel. I had discovered this when I first moved here. I had been thinking of importing French wines, because the only Israeli wines I knew about were the sweet ones used at holidays and the others that left you with a headache. My editor at *Link*, however, told me this was no longer true, and offered to introduce me to the country's wine revolutionaries. I was ecstatic. This would make a great story since, like me, most people were unaware of the development. We made arrangements to go, and David Perlmutter, my guide to the nooks and crannies of Israel, took us in his Isuzu Trooper to the Golan, the site of one of Israel's finest wineries.

David's air-conditioned jeep was comfortable—much more so than the forest ranger's open-air vehicle I'd explored in off-road in the Galilee. As we steadily climbed the black volcanic cliffs in the shadow of snow-covered Mount Hermon, David gave us a little

So simple and fragrant, wine has the irresistible power to attach itself to memory.

background. Several decades ago, a wine expert from California had persuaded the apple growers on the Golan Heights to switch their crop to grapes, citing the cool climate and excellent soil drainage of the Golan and Upper Galilee. So in 1976, the farmers hired winemakers from Napa Valley and planted their first vines. They harvested their grapes in the chill of the night in order to keep the grapes from mildewing and turning sour in the warm trucks on the way to be crushed at the winery—a procedure that contributes to the wine's crisp taste.

David Perlmutter

The Israeli wine revolution had barely begun in 1984 when the winery's first vintage was received with loud acclaim from the international wine community. I couldn't wait to try it. When we arrived at the winery's long wooden bar, our expedition tasted Yarden's full-bodied Cabernet Sauvignon and then a cold, fruity Sauvignon Blanc. The flavor of the wine was what I would expect from the finest California wine, not at all cooked or acidic. My editor was right. Israel's wine *was* wonderful. I bought an iced Blanc de Blanc to take with us for a picnic lunch, and David's four-wheel-drive took us off-road to a cool stream under shady trees. We sipped glasses of Israeli champagne accompanied by chunky chicken and walnut salad—a perfect meal for a perfect day.

Indeed our spontaneity and *joie de vivre* brought to mind the wonderful month in 1971 that Ted and I had spent driving through the countryside of France, impulsively dropping into chateaux without reservations. It was then I first began to take wine seriously.

In Saumur, we visited a winery high on the banks of the Loire River. Smelling of oak and sour fermentation, the dark and musty cave was crowded with vats, barrels, and rows of dusty bottles. Standing at a wooden bar, I was handed a glass of chilled sparkling white wine. Mimicking the others at the tasting, I first lifted the glass to my nose to breathe in the aroma, then sipped, delaying swallowing until my taste buds were saturated. The demi-sec was too sweet and cloying for me, but the extra brut danced on my tongue. We bought three bottles for eighteen francs, which amounted to four dollars, and put them into our ice chest. Then we drove until the view was just right and out came the crusty baguettes, slabs of local pâté, and wedges of cheese. The Reblochon, the Brie, and the Camembert were delicious, but my favorite was boursin au poivre, a chalky white, full-fat cheese rolled in crushed black peppercorns.

Drinking our cold wine in plastic footed flutes, Ted and I sat on a grass hillock breathing in the fresh air, enchanted by the little towns and churches tucked along the banks of the river lazily flowing at our feet. The fragrant Sancerre Sauvignon Blanc made such an impression on us that, many years later, when sailing to Saint Martin in the Caribbean, we recognized it in a wine-shop and loaded the boat with three cases to take home.

France's viticulture is a great tradition, but wine-making, I discovered, did not begin with the French. Quality wine had been produced in Phoenicia and in prebiblical Israel over two thousand years before the Greeks and Romans brought it to Europe. An official at the winery had told me there is evidence that wine was made near the Sea of Galilee as early as 6000 B.C. Some scholars also believe that Noah's ark came to rest in eastern Turkey, where he planted the first recorded vineyard in 3000 B.C.

Winemaking in ancient Israel reached its zenith during the time of the Second Temple, at the beginning of the Common Era. But wine practically disappeared from the region after the Arab conquest in the seventh century, when Muhammad prohibited alcohol and the vines were subsequently uprooted. It was not until the late 1800s that the Israeli wine industry was brought back to life, when Baron Edmond de Rothschild created the Carmel Winery. When Ted's grandfather participated in the baron's cooperative, he thus helped revive an ancient tradition, restoring the vineyards and producing wine after so many centuries of disuse.

Inevitably, I then visited the venerable sprawling Carmel Winery in Zichron. Like many of Israel's older wineries, it too had been influenced by the new standards of winemaking in Israel. To remain competitive, Carmel hired Gil Shatzberg as a winemaker. Gil was born in the community of Tzora, home of reputed winemaker Roni James. There, as a child, Gil discovered his love for winemaking. The Carmel Winery saw his potential and sent him to the University of California–Davis to study, and then to apprentice at the revered Jordan Winery in Napa Valley. The Jordan Winery was so impressed by Gil that they offered to buy his contract from the Carmel Winery. But Gil refused—he preferred to use his skills to enhance the wine industry in Israel.

When he returned from the States, Gil persuaded the veteran Carmel farmers to cut off some of the grapes in their vineyards and have them rot in the fields, thus allowing the remaining grapes to develop better quality. As an incentive, the growers were paid for a kilo even though they brought in six hundred grams of grapes. Because the farmers own the winery, Gil felt they would eventually make more money when the wine improved and could command higher prices.

Harvest time at the Tzora winery

Gil's efforts at Carmel were so successful that a consortium offered him financial backing to create his own winery. Gil's new enterprise now lies among two-thousand-year-old olive trees on Guy Rilov's vast Makura Ranch, just north of Zichron Yaacov, where Guy has been producing exquisite organic olive oil for years. Together, Guy's olive oil and Gil's new Amphorae wines—already leaders in a rapidly expanding industry—are a perfect match.

My search for Israel's leading winemakers eventually drew me to Yair Margalit. My editor had warned me that it was impossible to locate this revolutionary small winemaker. The first part, however, was surprisingly easy; he was listed in the telephone directory. But finding his winery was something else! It was buried in an orange grove between Netanya and Hadera—and there are countless orange groves in that area.

This time, I persuaded Ted to come along. We drove down dirt paths between orange trees, engulfed by a cloud of red dust, before finally arriving at an old, abandoned packing house covered in fuchsia and orange bougainvillea. Yair was standing on a ladder, hovering over an old-fashioned wooden-slatted press, his strong arms elbow-deep in the must of fermentation, kneading grape skins together with dark purple juice tinged with white flecks of yeast.

It was like watching a musician perform. His eyes were hooded in reverie, as if listening to the music of his own private muse. He turned the large metal screw to separate the juice from the skins. Beakers and tubing hung on the walls like at a chemistry lab; indeed, Margalit had been a chemist before he became captivated by winemaking. He had been taking chemistry courses at the University of California–Davis and studying winemaking as a hobby. When he came back to Israel, Jonathan Tishbi, owner of the Baron Winery, asked him to make their first vintage. Tishbi was more than satisfied with the result, but Margalit was not. He went back to Davis for further courses, and then opened the Margalit Winery upon his return.

Though Margalit had been a scientist, he uses his

Israel's fledgling Route du Vin is not like the established ones in central France, Strasbourg, or Napa Valley. Ben Zaken, Shatzberg, and Margalit stand out because they are innovators, even rebels. In time, society will catch up with their revolutionary ideas.

Gil Shatzberg with an eighty-seven-year-old winemaker

intuition as well as his senses to make wine. "Each year is different because of the rain and the amount of sun," he told Ted and me. "Wine is alive. When the grape is picked, instead of dying and disintegrating, it changes form and improves with age even in the bottle. I have to understand and work with its movement and transformation."

A tractor in Dalton Winery

Margalit has, indeed, succeeded. At a blind tasting in Paris, Margalit ranked just behind Chateau Mouton Rothschild, Lafite Rothschild, Latour, and Haut Brion, with 86 out of 100 points.

Ted and I sat with Yair under his orange trees, sipping a 1993 Cabernet Sauvignon and nibbling borekas, cheese puffs wrapped in filo dough that Yair heated in a small toaster oven. The wine, food, and freedom from the constraints of our schedules all reminded us of our trips into the French countryside when we were young and carefree.

Meeting Israel's up-and-coming vintners had been an inspiration. I had started on the open road as a professional dream gatherer and discovered some very practical visionaries: intellectual dreamers up to their elbows in fermentation, patiently coaxing nature's bounty from a noble, ancient land. Although I had launched my frenetic forays from Tel Aviv as a reporter, the stories had become part of me. I had been writing myself into this Mediterranean clime unawares. Like the wine I'd been learning about, I had been personally fermenting over the years, becoming more patient, more confident. Increasingly I realized I was more than a tourist to these places: I was becoming an Israeli-American. Not only that, but I'd reemerged and was myself again—and feeling good about it.

Ben Zaken, Shatzberg, and Margalit could hire people to make their wine, but they prefer to put their own hands into the grapes and feel them. As these revolutionary men revealed to me, winemaking is best conducted with loving hearts and informed hands. Then patience is needed—time for fermentation—and finally, trust. Winemakers must trust in the future, observing the climatic changes, then adding or subtracting, working and waiting, depending on the conditions. These vintners create art. They are like painters, composers, and poets. They decant their dreams.

Yair Margalit in his winery

CHAPTER TWELVE

Around the Corner

The gypsy in me was forced to come to a halt for a while. My wish to stay still long enough to watch the buds unfold—to witness the cycles of each season—was fulfilled under sad circumstances. Ted became ill, and for a year was in and out of the hospital just two blocks from our apartment in Tel Aviv. I sat with him in various rooms in the hospital—first a small white cubicle, its windows overlooking a garden of newly planted trees and flower beds; then a dark minuscule room where we climbed over equipment; and later a larger room with windows that overlooked the nurses' station and rows of beds in intensive care.

Not wanting to be far from him, I stopped driving to my special haunts. Hospital vigils take their toll, so when I needed fresh air and some exercise I began exploring the streets nearby. At first I ventured just a few blocks, but as I felt more secure that Ted was responding well to his treatments, my forays became longer. The streets were lined with either monotonous apartments on

My motto is "turn lemons into lemonade," but Ted's illness proved quite a challenge in that regard.

Jacaranda tree

stilts, all covered with years of grime, or newer office buildings. Yet I hardly noticed them. I was imprisoned by my own fears and barely conscious of a life outside the hospital. I developed a routine, first walking down tree-lined King David Boulevard and past our apartment building before coming to the tacky main street of Ibn Gvirol. In my car, I had raced away from this shoddy street, instead driving farther north, where I'd found solace in the open road and the little Mediterranean seaside villages that dotted it. Now, instead of driving, I merely plodded past.

Market in Tel Aviv

One day, however, I inexplicably turned onto the street and actually covered on foot the entire distance of Ibn Gvirol—to the blue metal bridge that spanned the Yarkon River and back. Curiously, I began to examine each store window. Although it was a hot, sunny day, I'd stayed cool due to the shady loggia that covered the sidewalk. I soon realized that when I had previously driven by, the pillars of the loggia had shadowed the store window displays. But now the shade enticed me to peer into the shop windows. I was grateful to the architect who had prioritized human needs over aesthetic appearance.

As I sat in one of the coffeehouses along the strip, sipping an icy espresso through a long straw, I mentally redecorated the seedy supporting pillars, imagining them to be adorned with colorful, painted designs and artistic mosaics. Pleased with the "results," I realized that Ibn Gvirol could be both comfortable and visually interesting.

Several minutes later I experienced déjà vu. Opposite me, three- and four-story residential dwellings rose above shops, just as they had in my childhood neighborhood of Washington Heights. Although those in New York were faced with red brick, Tel Aviv's dwellings had facades of warm-climate beige stucco, like those in Miami. Suddenly, Tel Aviv appeared as a combination of both my former homes.

The apartments and shops in Tel Aviv also looked like the ones depicted in the painting of New York that hung above my bed. Our 1928 painting by Burliuk pictured pushcarts, old-fashioned automobiles, and fire escapes scaling three- and four-story buildings. Next to it hung a stylized Gropper charcoal drawing of fire escapes and signs over shops— "Dentist," "Tailor," "Rooms-to-Let," "Baths," "For Sale"—and women on the street below wearing babushkas and cats scraping for food in the metal garbage cans.

I soon found other things oddly familiar. As I continued up Ibn Gvirol, the smell of rotisserie chicken and aroma of pickles reminded me of Sundays in New York. With my small hand enveloped by my father's, I would often accompany him for Sunday-morning brunch on the Lower East Side. I liked the potato knishes much more than the kasha, made from nutritious buckwheat and too healthful for my childish taste. And sitting at a table in Katz's delicatessen, the stuffed derma and gravy had been a rare and unhealthful treat.

Streets of Tel Aviv

Poinciana tree

Once I became more open to Tel Aviv, I began to notice the trees as well. A fernlike canopy shaded a strip of garden on one side of King David Boulevard. Although the feathery leaves all looked the same, the varied textures of the trunks and the astonishing variety of blooms in May and June suggested otherwise. Purple trumpets of jacaranda heralded the arrival of the yellow thumb-sized orchids characteristic of the Mouth of the Lion, which in turn were followed by large, flame-orange poinciana that filled the sky with fiery flashes of spring. In Miami I'd had to drive twenty minutes to enjoy a boulevard filled with poinciana; in Tel Aviv it was but a block away.

The greenery and lush flowers conjured up memories of the park where I'd spent so much time as a child.

To escape the cramped confines of my family's apartment, I often sought refuge in walking. I was drawn to the peaceful gardens of Fort Tryon Park, even entranced by the pebbles in the paths between the flower beds. In the park across the street from our apartment, my friends and I took the sycamore pods that fell to the ground and split them into wings to wear on our noses. Later, when I took my son, Michael, and Sarah, one of his daughters, to the neighborhood and taught them how to play with sycamore pods, they giggled as they pranced on the grass of my childhood jungle and sat on the rock throne in my fairy-tale park.

Tel Aviv was unexpectedly growing on me. Soon I discovered a place that would become a favorite: a café filled with wooden chairs, wrought-iron three-legged tables with cracked plastic tops decorated with printed leaves, an old wooden floor, and, most notably, a silver espresso machine topped by an Italian eagle with outstretched wings.

The café overlooked a small garden bordered by sidewalks populated with *Ficus religiosa* trees—considered holy in Nepal. Their heart-shaped leaves sprouted tails that wagged downward and would eventually bear figs. I glanced upward at one with Ted in mind. I had learned that these trees are also called bo or Bodhi trees in India, and they are regarded there, too, as sacred and a sign of enlightenment. I looked to see if there were figs on the tree before realizing that figs were out of season. Searching for a ray of hope, needing comfort about Ted's health, I decided to check again toward the end of the summer.

On Saturdays the streets emptied of cars and a gentle hush settled over the offices. But Ted and I found no peace; illness knows no weekends. To escape from the hospital one Saturday, I chose a café on the other side of the garden in Masaryk Square, known for its oversized chocolate popovers—perfect comfort food. I was embarrassed at my need to escape into sugar, but the large pastry brought a little joy to my day. I ordered a large coffee as well and found myself steeped in memories. Years ago, Ted and I had been served our morning coffee in similar gigantic ceramic cups at the LeYaca Hotel in Saint-Tropez . . . .

I sipped my coffee and savored the chocolate treat, listening to the buzz of Hebrew at the next table. Although I was alone, I no longer felt isolated. I did not understand the words, but the familiar sound of the language calmed me. Appreciative of the city and renewed in ways that I did not fully comprehend, I returned to the hospital room better able to comfort Ted.

CHAPTER THIRTEEN

My Studio

Refuge at Home

When Ted was discharged from the hospital to continue his recovery at home, our apartment became an intensive care unit. Doctors, nurses, and physiotherapists attended to him at all hours of the day and night. We even dismantled our bedroom to accommodate his hospital bed.

I thought I would sleep right next to him on a cot. But the nurse dissuaded me, saying, "You won't get any sleep at all." I began sleeping on the couch in the living room. But soon the doctors advised against that, too. "Recovery will take a long time," they reminded me gently. "You need privacy and a proper place to sleep."

Fortunately, I didn't have to look too far: Ted and I had recently bought a two-bedroom apartment in our building. I had needed a bigger office than the tiny room in our apartment, where I could write and store my archives. I'd already filled the two bedrooms with invisible built-in file cabinets, designed by a clever Israeli to hold thirty years' worth of a pack rat and travel writer's papers. So I added a bed to the living room/writing area.

The studio quickly became my haven. After kissing Ted good night every evening, I would escape from the medical monitors to my quiet refuge downstairs.

Almond trees in blossom, Nahal Dishon

The studio was on the first floor, close enough to smell the freshly mown grass in the morning. In the middle of the night, I didn't turn on the light; feeling the cool stone of the tile under my bare feet, I would reach out blindly, navigating my way with the fossilized granite of the countertops hard under my fingertips. In a primitive way, the studio became mine when I roamed it in darkness.

After I awoke at dawn, I would step onto the smooth golden stones of my rear terrace. As I breathed in eucalyptus and pine, I watched the ubiquitous brown sparrows fly to the tops of the old trees that stood adjacent to our apartment, where Ted was recuperating. The beautiful mornings reminded me of being in Athens with Ted, where I'd danced in the golden light that reflected off the worn stones at the Acropolis.

The sunset's gentle glow recalled a trip I had taken to the Galilee. There, the last light of day had disappeared with a hush, leaving the worn stones of the ancient synagogue of Gush Halav and the mountainside rising behind them in softness. I remembered how our jeep had eased down a narrow dirt road; as shadows filled the dry riverbed of Nahal Dalton, ghostly pale almond trees growing along the embankment showed the way. Such Mediterranean reveries in my studio prepared me for the more difficult Tel Aviv days ahead.

I also found unexpected comfort in furnishing my studio with whimsical, spontaneous purchases: toys. On my walks, I began picking up bits and pieces in the neighborhood. Walking past a toy store, a soft floppy frog dressed in green paisley caught my eye, and I impulsively dashed in to buy it. With the parcel under my arm, I left the store . . . but was stopped by the soulful stare of a whimsical rocking horse in the window. Back into the toy store I went. Hand-carved in hard wood and gaily painted in Thailand, the rocking horse was of the same genre as the banana trees and cartoon-like fruit Ted and I had brought back from cruising in Southeast Asia. I decided this lively steed would carry my frog at a gallop around my workplace.

Another toy store displayed in its window a colorful hot-air balloon with the words "Around the World" emblazoned on its side. A camera-toting clown—his toes poking out of worn shoes—sat in the basket. Of course, I had to have it, and it swings from the ceiling in my entranceway. Small metal windup toys were next: a butterfly, a seal balancing a ball on its nose, a monkey on a tricycle, a singing chicken with three chickadees, and a hopping parrot. I wound them up to keep me company. Then I furnished my desk with three papier-mâché dancers in colorful leotards, sculpted in the Nana style of Niki Saint-Phalle. I later added several soft baby-doll beanbags with glass eyes and intelligent faces, which reminded me of my

Though Ted and I continued to act as if we were alone, trying to ignore the constantly present medical attention, even our good-night kisses were not in private. While the nurses were sensitive to our needs, they could not change the reality of the demands of his illness.

Ancient synagogue in Gush Halav, Israel

Although the studio was not set up for dining, to my delight, even Ted enjoyed having lunch with me there. I only wished his visits could be more frequent and longer. His attention flattered me. Though he was ill, our romance remained healthy.

grandchildren. Perched on the edge of my bookshelves, they could watch over me.

But I didn't stop there. I placed above my computer a collection of four fishing animals: a green dragon, a purple elephant, a gold- and orange-spotted giraffe, and a green-eyed sheep. Instead of fish, two lemons, an eggplant, and a strawberry dangled at the end of their lines. Then my family got involved, too, when my young grandson Daniel brought me a Minnie Mouse from Disney World. He'd also given Ted a Mickey Mouse, but I absconded with it so that Mickey and Minnie could sit together on my shelf.

The toys in the studio lightened the atmosphere and assuaged my loneliness. I found myself laughing when I entered it, and my friends and family also seemed lighthearted when they visited. I had never been a toy collector; having so many toys around was totally unplanned. Surrounded by grinning toys allowed me to think the space was not serious and waylaid my fears of writing.

I was surprised by how attached I'd become to my studio. Years ago, I had attempted to purchase a two-story terraced house in Jaffa, situated on bluffs above the Mediterranean—an idyllic creative haven. I'd been enthralled by the roar of the waves and the spray of the sea and was betting that the surrounding dilapidated neighborhood would eventually turn around.

The owner had first agreed to sell, but then the family could not part with their home. I still regret not sitting out on the terrace overlooking the sea, but I know that I would have not driven to Jaffa at night. More important, it would not have been as convenient during Ted's illness as my present studio.

I use my studio at all hours, padding in a white terry-cloth robe past the knowing concierge in the lobby to slip into my hideaway. Over the years, the walls have slowly become a little more decorous. Along with my toys, my studio now contains a glorious oil painting by a German master from Jerusalem, which realistically depicts the Jaffa marketplace of the late nineteenth century. It fills a wall of my airy living room–cum–writing space; floor-to-ceiling bookcases fill two other large walls. Neil Folberg's photographs of feluccas, sailboats on the Nile, slate roofs in Yugoslavia, and olive trees in the Galilee are also prominent fixtures. Someday, I hope to find a sensuous Moroccan divan to complete the setting.

Maybe one day I'll have another studio in a seaside apartment in Herzliya. With our boat docked in the marina below, I could always be ready to sail off in gypsy fashion. As sea spray misted my face, I'd write on the terrace in Herzliya, listening to the sound of the waves pounding on the beach as I did in Miami. With Ted ill, however, my current refuge was perfect.

Nahal Tabor, Galilee

CHAPTER FOURTEEN

Tel Aviv

Transformed

E ven with Ted out of the hospital for several months, I no longer felt the need to drive away from the labyrinthine streets of my neighborhood. As I picked my way through the maze of small buildings, I found they now gave me my bearings, while century-old tall trees on the sidewalks offered shade. One of my favorite destinations soon became the artistic neighborhood of Neve Tzedek, a Mediterranean village in the heart of Tel Aviv. My niece Talia had introduced me to it ten years ago. From the outskirts Neve Tzedek had appeared forbidding, nestled behind a dilapidated row of houses that faced the beach. But I was taken by the miracle of the Suzanne Dellal Center: Located in the heart of rampant decay, it contained a plaza of orange trees, their painted white trunks eerily luminescent in the artificial light. The soothing sound of flowing water filled the night air as we entered one of the two-story buildings to watch a modern dance performance.

The clay woman and I now relax on the front terrace of my studio. Together, we overlook the sparkling blue swimming pool, considering rather lackadaisically whether we should plunge in and exercise. So far, both of us have successfully ignored the nagging idea.

View to Tel Aviv from Jaffa

Over one hundred years ago, a tiny group of Jews had built Neve Tzedek on the sand dunes beside the Mediterranean after being forced out of Jaffa by overcrowding and disease. As the years passed, it became obvious to Zev Sokolowski, a young visionary, that the villagers' one-story, terra-cotta-roofed homes were rotting and badly in need of repair. So he persuaded his in-laws to fund the renovation of two small, historic schools to create the Suzanne Dellal Center of Theatre and Dance. This became the catalyst for the renovation of the whole neighborhood. Soon artists' studios, boutiques, cafés, restaurants, and low apartment buildings began to emerge.

One day near the Suzanne Dellal Center on Shabazi Street, I stumbled upon Iris Dishon. A striking woman with a wild mane of strawberry-red hair and peaceful, light green eyes, she painted on fabric to create unique furniture in her atelier. I purchased four chairs from her; they now sit around a metal table in my studio, their individualistic still-life renditions of fruit a delight.

One day while exploring in Neve Tzedek, I saw a clay sculpture of a woman—with sagging breasts and belly—through a locked wrought-iron gate in front of the Rokach House, a local museum. Intrigued, I photographed the woman. Several years later, when I brought our friends to the Rokach House for Ted's seventy-fifth birthday celebration, I met Lea Majaro-Mintz, the soft-spoken sculptress. Lea's grandfather, Shimon Rokach, had founded Neve Tzedek. Painstakingly and without help, Lea had restored her grandfather's home into a museum in order to pay tribute to the town's origins. Rokach House now displays film, old photographs, artifacts, and, most touchingly, Lea's grandmother's wedding dress, sewn from batiste undergarments brought from Europe. The museum is also a gallery of Lea's art. When I visited again with our friends, I saw that the clay woman was still

Lea Majaro-Mintz

The Bat Sheva Dance group's studio, Neve Tzedek, Tel Aviv

sitting on the steps out front. Unable to resist, I brought her home with me.

Neve Tzedek was not the only area of Tel Aviv I grew to appreciate. I also began to walk past my garden and the cafés on Masaryk Square to King George Street. Red paper lanterns hung in the trees in front of a dim-sum restaurant. I waved to the cordial proprietor of a small antique furniture store, who sold me a wooden rocking chair with two carved elephants on each side, their trunks searching the air, perhaps for peanuts. I had stored it in my closet, but planned to give it to my brother in the States for his grandchild. (He has one grandchild so far and I have nine.)

Along the way, in front of Pollak's antique prints and book store, I encountered the circle of sycamores that the artist Rubin had saved from demolition. The enormous dome of verdant leaves offered me solace in the summer heat. I looked to the other old sycamores in the park across the street. Their seedpods reminded me of the wings my son, grand-daughter, and I had "flown" on in our visit to my childhood park. In my reverie, I smiled at the babies being pushed in their prams. It seemed that history was repeating itself. But if history repeats itself in gentle ways, it eventually also unfolds in less pleasant certainties.

CHAPTER FIFTEEN

Ted's Birthday Party

My Coming Out

After successfully battling three outbreaks of two kinds of cancer over a four-year period, Ted felt like celebrating. Though still plagued with other illnesses, he was overjoyed at returning to life and wanted to share his delight at having won his latest struggle with death. "I want a big birthday party when I turn seventy-five," he told me. "I want to invite friends and family from all over the world who have made a difference in my life."

He also wished to celebrate the remarkable achievements he'd accomplished during our decade in Israel. Ted wanted to integrate our two worlds by introducing our Israeli family, friends, business associates, ministers of government—even the prime minister—to our friends and family from abroad.

I had to make that party happen. Ted's latest brush with death, however, had occurred only several weeks before, and I was afraid that he might not survive the next two and a half months until his birthday. Still, I threw myself into the planning, because I knew his anticipation of something

Ted knew a party would be very draining, but his desire to celebrate and live life to the fullest took precedence over his diminished physical resources. A risk-taker, he understood and had the strength of character to accept the consequences.

Wildflowers in Golan

wonderful would certainly help his recuperation. There is a very fine line between self-definition and self-confidence. Although fragile, Ted was still facing challenges and goals. I wanted him to be able to continue to be himself, and my job was to see to it that it taxed his health as little as possible.

I had not planned any large parties since Ted's cancer had first surfaced four years earlier, but I knew I could pull it off successfully. This celebration would be a surprise for our Israeli friends, as they had not seen me in the role of major party planner and international hostess. The presence of foreign guests meant that this event had to be conducted in English, as are all international events in Israel. Ironically, my functioning in English thus turned out to be an advantage.

I chartered a plane to bring our friends from abroad and arranged for them to stay for a week in order to get over the jet lag and make the long flight worthwhile. This was my chance to introduce them to Ted's unpublicized past, the Israel of Ted's youth, as well as to the modern Israel in which he had become a successful participant. I looked forward to sharing my Israel, too. I knew some of my favorite nooks and crannies, which I had written about as a journalist, would provide refreshing insights even for the seasoned traveler: Lea Majaro-Mintz's Rokach House in Neve Tzedek; Neil Folberg and his Vision Gallery in Jerusalem's Nahalat Shiva; Esther Rubin, who would introduce the paintings of old Tel Aviv in the Rubin Museum; and a performance of the Bat Sheva Dance Group at the Suzanne Dellal Center in Neve Tzedek.

To prepare them for the adventures that lay ahead, I tucked a video into their welcome-to-Israel kits. From

Lea Majaro-Mintz's Rokach House in Neve Tzedek

that, our guests learned that at age eleven, Ted—wearing short pants and looking very innocent—had run guns for the Israeli underground, smuggling a revolver in a bouquet of flowers right under the noses of the occupying British army. They also learned that later, while he was in the Jewish Brigade of the British army in World War II, Ted had helped inmates of concentration camps make their clandestine way to Israel.

The day before the grand party, I brought three busloads of our friends to Zichron Yaacov and proudly showed them Grandfather Moshe's barn. In the booklet from the Pioneer Museum, they read stories about Ted's father and realized how much Ted's risk-taking resembled his father's and grandfather's boldness. There, Ted also pointed out photographs of his family to our grandchildren. We all lunched at Pastoraly, a delightful restaurant in a farmer's courtyard, owned and restored by one of Ted's cousins. The restaurant's décor included old photographs of the pioneer families and even one of

Grandfather Moshe's barn

Stream in Nahal Tabor

Ted and his sisters when they were children. Ted was surprised he was part of a historical exhibit, but despite his modesty, he was secretly pleased: He saw himself portrayed as an essential part of Israel's communal past, in which he'd had the privilege of participating. I could not have been more proud of my husband.

After lunch, I brought our friends to the founders' wall and shared the story of my first visit to Zichron. "This is where the family history started," I told them. This Mediterranean village, which I had adopted from Ted, had become so dear to me. Although this was to be primarily Ted's celebration, it represented us as a couple. We had spent a third of our married life together in Israel and I realized that I also had much to say about it.

For Ted it was a week in which he had to marshal his resources, participating in whatever touring and party events seemed most appropriate. He enjoyed the dance performance at Neve Tzedek and dinner at Erez, a rustic restaurant in Herzliya that turned out the most delicious bread as well as pizza cooked in a stone wood-burning oven. One evening, Ted arrived at Picasso's in Herzliya when the party was already in full swing. We had turned the restaurant into a pub, and everyone was dancing on the tables. Not to be outdone, Ted climbed up on a table, pulling his daughter, Shari, and me with him. We have wonderful pictures of him dancing with gusto. Before coming to Picasso's he had been exhausted, but the nurses had rallied him; the Israeli music and his courageous heritage gave him the strength to lead the joyous celebration.

I also engaged David Perlmutter to head a group of guides who offered many touring options during the rest of the week, so that all our guests could tailor their Israeli experience to their tastes—and previous visits, if any. We presented several different options to our foreign guests—who were not all Jewish—to explore Jerusalem, Caesarea, Acco, Nazareth, and the Galilee. And Michael Stern, the producer of the week-long celebration, creatively interpreted and implemented my guidelines, teaching me that Israel had much to offer in artistic management.

Ted had never let illness hold him back. In 1997, while hospitalized in New York's Memorial Sloan-Kettering Hospital for throat cancer, he had decided to travel to Miami to thank our friends for financially supporting the American contingent to the Maccabiah, the Jewish Olympics held in Israel every four years. The children and I thought he was crazy. "Why not film a video thanking them?" we asked. "Or how about a simulcast?" For Ted, though, nothing would do but flying in person to the gala. Once there, he took the stage in a wheelchair to whisper his thank-yous. Everyone was moved. The Maccabians went beyond themselves to achieve their athletic feats, and Ted Arison was also that kind of person. He pushed beyond the limits, and in doing so, he enabled all of us who were touched by him to become bigger people.

For our final, dramatic adventure we gathered in the spectacular Judean desert. Our caravan of jeeps snaked through the desert for a picnic luncheon on a carpet spread upon the sand, overlooking a ravine in which Mar Saba, an azure-domed monastery, was located. That evening we brought the desert theme to the sea. Our ever-attentive crew, wearing flowing white galabias and matching turbans, graciously welcomed us aboard our yacht—the *Mylin IV*, illuminated in warm, soft candlelight. The crew might have been the shepherds we had seen that day leading their sheep over the wide expanse of desert sand dunes. Even for the guests who lived in great palazzos, it was a very powerful experience. Somehow a yacht that crosses the sea to foreign lands carries with it its own special mystique. We had entertained large groups on the *Mylin* in Europe and the States, but never in Israel. Our friends from abroad were entranced with the romantic coastline—framed in darkness, lights flickering.

I always had wished to integrate our old Miami life into our new Israeli one, but had no way of doing it until Ted's celebration. I never expected it would happen in Israel. During the evening of the birthday party itself, the Israelis and foreign guests formed a harmonious whole. The catering hall—a building with glass walls set in an open, rolling field near Herzliya—was transformed into a lavish Moroccan tent. We had racks of glittering gossamer caftans and galabias, and dressers to cajole the party-goers into donning them over their formalwear. If I had declared it to be a masquerade party, the Israelis would have felt too self-conscious to participate. This way, everyone had a drink, relaxed, and became involved in the event, including the costumes. Thanks to the oriental music's melodic and insistent beat, the dancing did not cease until early morning. In sparkling robes, striking headdresses, baubles, and beads, everyone looked equally festive. There was no noticeable difference between outsiders and insiders; all the guests melded together, happily celebrating Ted's life and their relationships with him.

Ted, ill as he was, was participating fully. Wearing his galabia, he sat in a comfortable upholstered chair next to the dance floor, welcoming his friends and family who, one by one, offered him warm wishes. Our security guards warned the guests not to shake Ted's hand or hug him because he bruised so easily, but many could not resist. Even though he was forced to remain seated, his irrepressible charm and strong presence drew everyone to him. Earlier, he had told the nurses he would just make an appearance

Preparing for the picnic luncheon overlooking Mar Saba

Osim Tsiltum

Aboard the Mylin IV *with the coast in the distance*

and would leave by nine o'clock. We stayed until midnight. It was obvious to everyone that Ted was enjoying his party enormously.

On an impulse, I stopped the music, walked onto the stage, and called up all our children and grandchildren—Ted's, who over the years had become mine, and my son, Michael, who had become Ted's—and we led the guests in singing "Happy Birthday." Ted just beamed at his proud and joyous family.

Our friends from abroad had enjoyed a full week of richly varied happenings. They had met our Israeli friends, businesspeople, politicians, and artists. My discovery of Mediterranean Israel enabled them to experience an Israel unknown to the average tourist. Our guests left marveling at the comfort of their stay and their ability to experience Israel from a new vantage point. Ted was thrilled, too. "This is what I wanted, and I got it," he said. His appreciation was my fulfilling reward.

Rose petal fountain

Ted's dreams didn't stop with the birthday party. Though ill, he continued to be himself—energetic and visionary. He dragged us to Prague, where he introduced the president of his bank and the head of his construction company to the Eastern bloc, which was ripe for expansion. He then flew his business associates to the *Mylin* in the Seychelles, where Ted proceeded to teach them his specialty— fishing enormous fighting tuna. Our fish chest was overflowing. In the Seychelles, however, overwhelmed by the heat, humidity, and unrelenting pace, Ted became ill. After two nightmarish months of hospitalization in intensive care for heart failure and pneumonia, he decided to continue his recuperation aboard the *Mylin* in Saint-Tropez. Even his doctors encouraged his insatiable will to participate in life. I should have seen what was coming—but the strength of his person masked the intensity of his illness.

Women married to creative men tend to become part of their creations. Ted named our yachts after me. He created the Mylin IV, *our last boat that enabled him to do what he enjoyed most— traversing the sea to experience new lands. He had incorporated into the* Mylin *all the art and skill he had acquired in constructing cruise ships. It was the personal expression of his professional self, and his gesture of naming it after me is a compliment that I will always cherish.*

CHAPTER SIXTEEN

In Mourning
Love Survives

A month after our trip to Saint-Tropez, my husband died. After the shock of Ted's death began to subside, I went to Tucson, Arizona, to continue healing. The hiking, the healthful food, nature, massages, the behavioral therapist dealing with grief and loss, touch and healing . . . all of these helped. I hiked up a narrow sandy trail, high upon an Arizona mountain, watching my feet step one in front of the other. When my hiking guide stopped to point out a soaring wall of rock that jutted into the crisp clear sky, I appreciated its beauty but missed the more beautiful formations in Israel—the turquoise and pink primordial rock, millions of years old.

My guide had told me the desert mountains of Israel are most like those of Tucson, and I wanted to learn about those similarities. At the bottom of the Tucson gorge were a line of smooth, round rocks where thousands of years ago the Native Americans had cooked their food. As an American who greatly enjoys food, I should have been able to identify, but somehow I did not.

Israel was small and intimate; I felt connected there. Israel was where I had been living and loving.

Poppies and olive trees, Nahal Zalmon, Israel

Instead, I discovered that the stones that marked the Jewish people's migration from Mesopotamia to Israel had drawn me far from this American landscape that had once held such an attraction for me.

When we paused at a steep cliff to eat our breakfast, a herd of javalina—wild boar the size of large dogs—headed up the mountain opposite us. My guide was overwhelmed at the rare sight. Although I was moved, I envisioned the frisky gazelles I had seen leaping across the desert rocks in Eilat. The gazelles in Israel—their pert white tails like cotton balls—were more mine than the javalina, which I was merely visiting. As a souvenir of my encounter with the javalina/gazelles, I picked up a small, jagged rose quartz stone. Later, I affixed it to a hiking stick made from the rib of a saguaro cactus that had withered in Arizona's Sonoran Desert, leaving its wooden skeleton standing erect, sturdy yet light.

Much to my surprise, I was hungry to return to Israel to begin hiking seriously. I had written my travel articles so that both Israelis and visitors to Israel would be enticed to venture into the wilderness. But I myself had traveled to Israel's beautiful geological sites mostly by jeep. Until now, I had hiked extensively in Tucson and not much in Israel, where the terrain seemed too rugged.

As in the Galápagos, nature engaged me and revealed my next step. This time, however, it engaged me in a negative way: As beautiful as it was, I no longer felt at home in Arizona. It was part of an America that had become too vast and impersonal for me. Arizona was beautiful, but I felt like a wanderer.

The hiking staff I was bringing home with me to Israel would remind me of Arizona's geographical splendor. I could hike holding my sturdy and practical walking stick in my hand—unlike my childhood years, when I'd grabbed the string that held my imaginary dog, Tivoli. With my feet on the ground, climbing trails into the Israeli mountains, I might begin to compensate for my true loss—one much greater than losing my Sleepyhead doll or my cherished Miami, a far greater one that would painfully accompany me everywhere.

I returned to Israel for the first time without Ted. The coastline was gray and brooding, clouded in dirt-colored rain, the bleak Mediterranean no more than a brown and muddy slough. Tel Aviv itself lay small, flat, and stained in sediment. My stomach fell. What was I thinking when I looked forward to a comforting return? Was my love of Israel only a product of my imagination? How could I feel so miserable if what I had been writing about over the years was real? In the car, crowded by my luggage, I tried to smile. As soon as I got home, however, I crawled under the covers, hiding from the invading melancholy of culture shock and feelings of loss.

Nahal Zalmon

Several days later the rain was still pelting the drab city, but I donned an all-weather coat and drove north. I had traveled these roads before. I turned right off the coastal road past the entrance to Zichron Yaacov in the Carmel Mountains and worked my way east toward the mountains of the Galilee, where ancient groves of olive trees stood stolid and timeless. As I navigated, the windshield wipers worked steadily to keep the road visible, revealing patchworks of

Olive trees, Galilee

young trees, rooted and surviving the elements. I, however, was looking for the older trees.

In the drenching rain, I found them. They were deeply rooted and stoic, just as I remembered. I sat in the car as the rain beat steadily upon the roof and stared at them. Standing by the wayside, these venerable trees exuded strength. They held their ground, still and strong for hundreds of years, resilient, their shallow root system continuously traveling long distances for nourishment. The older, the more gnarled and wounded, the more beautiful; they celebrated aging and life. The olive trees did not deny loss—as I knew I could not—but instead incorporated it into gentle new growth.

New growth brings with it memories and becomes part of who we are. As I sat in the pouring rain, I remembered a sunny day long ago on my first visit to Israel when Ted had taught me how to cut open an orange the Israeli way. We were driving up the coastal road when he abruptly swung the car across the highway and headed into a citrus grove, coming to a stop under an orange tree. As if entitled, he plucked a fruit from the tree, took out his small silver penknife, and inscribed a circle into the pocked skin around the stem. The sweet smell of citrus exploded into the stifling orchard. With the knife, he surgically marked equidistant longitudinal cuts.

Not long after my solitary trip, another experience unexpectedly soothed my pain: a very frightening midnight eye emergency that took me to Ichilov Hospital. It felt good to be welcomed by old friends. Doctors and nurses who had so lovingly ministered to Ted now gently cared for me. It reassured me that there was a foundation for new growth over old wounds.

Olive groves, Galil

Olive tree, Nahal Zalmon

Even though parts
of me had died with
Ted—leaving me
fragile, with a
gnawing emptiness—
over time I, like
the olive tree, could
grow new and tender
shoots around this
wound that was still
so fresh and raw.

With his fingers, he lifted the skin off the bursting fruit, then separated a section and offered it to me. The smell of the earth, the juice, and my tongue tasting the fruit were his wordless introduction to Israel. We were comfortable and fulfilled in the quietness.

My successful search through the torrents of rain for my olive trees gave me added strength and sufficient equilibrium to appreciate my life as a Mediterranean narrative. I still felt the void of Ted's absence—an enforced, painful silence—but now I also experienced the quiet peacefulness of reconnection. Although I was alone, my aloneness was not the oppressive silence of loneliness but rather the solitude of return.

Soon after, on the first anniversary of Ted's weeklong seventy-fifth birthday party, our family and friends relived the memories of the celebration. On the very day of his birthday, I discovered myself driving in the neighborhood of the cemetery. Spontaneously, I stopped. A man was selling flowers in a nearby wooden shed, so I bought bunches of miniature golden daffodils to bring Ted the harbingers of spring. The flowers reminded me of our last cruise on the *Mylin* in the south of France. Ted could not walk the country roads through the vineyards to the beach, as was our habit, so I walked them for him, bringing him the perfumed honeysuckle that wound its vines through fences along the way. The sunlight had warmed my face as I retraced our steps together. In the cemetery, I sat on the empty stone slab next to Ted's grave, comforted by his strong presence and the joy we had shared—a joy full of courage and life.

Although I am alone in Tel Aviv, the sun is shining again as the two coral trees in the garden under the apartment bloom in red jagged clusters of flowers. The shaggy eucalyptus still hosts its lively gaggle of birds as my neighboring boulevard prepares to turn purple with jacaranda, followed by the buttery yellow of the Mouth of the Lion and riotous orange when, in turn, the poinciana replace them. Soon the Indian sesame trees will trail their willowlike limbs, surrounded by lush masses of rosemary all interspersed with reeds like cat-o'-nine-tails. Colorful bougainvillea will soon sniff the breezes; lavender wisteria will climb the wooden arbor; and the pomegranates will flower in their appointed season.

I no longer sleep in my studio—in our apartment, the intensive care unit has been transformed back into a bedroom. Without Ted, the apartment feels empty. I try to fill it with daily routine, but it's not enough. I find myself at the Parisian café at Masaryk Square. After being shut for renovation, it once again receives me. I feel a palpable relief in the continuity. Beneath the green canopy of heart-shaped ficus leaves, next to the silvery convolutions of the strong trunk that supports them, I quietly sip a cup of coffee. The strong espresso comforts me. Enormous chocolate popovers decorate the window of the neighboring café. The hum of traffic fills the streets . . . and soon I shall turn to go home.

Tel Aviv, 2000

I'm back at Blue in my favorite corner overlooking the sea. It's November and yet there are still sunbathers basking on the sand and bare-chested men fishing on the jetty. The weather is similar in Miami, where I recently bought a small apartment on the beach. It has a terrace where I can sit and write, hearing the sound of the waves pounding on the beach and smelling the sea brine on tropical breezes. I plan to spend a few winter months there each year watching the sun rise over the ocean, enjoying my American grandchildren and family. The rest of the year, I expect to be here, in Tel Aviv, with my Israeli grandchildren and family, admiring the sun setting over the sea. As upside down as all this sounds, it no longer feels that way to me. I seem to have found my balance, a balance that even includes visiting places in between. During the past summer, I stumbled on a little village in France just north of Paris. It drew me to it and then invited me to return. As with Rosh Pina, I have enthusiastically responded. This village has fine art, traditional food, and intriguing stories. Curiously, the art even has roots in Mediterranean France.

As I move forward, patterns repeat in impressionistic hues, and, of course, I plan to write about it.

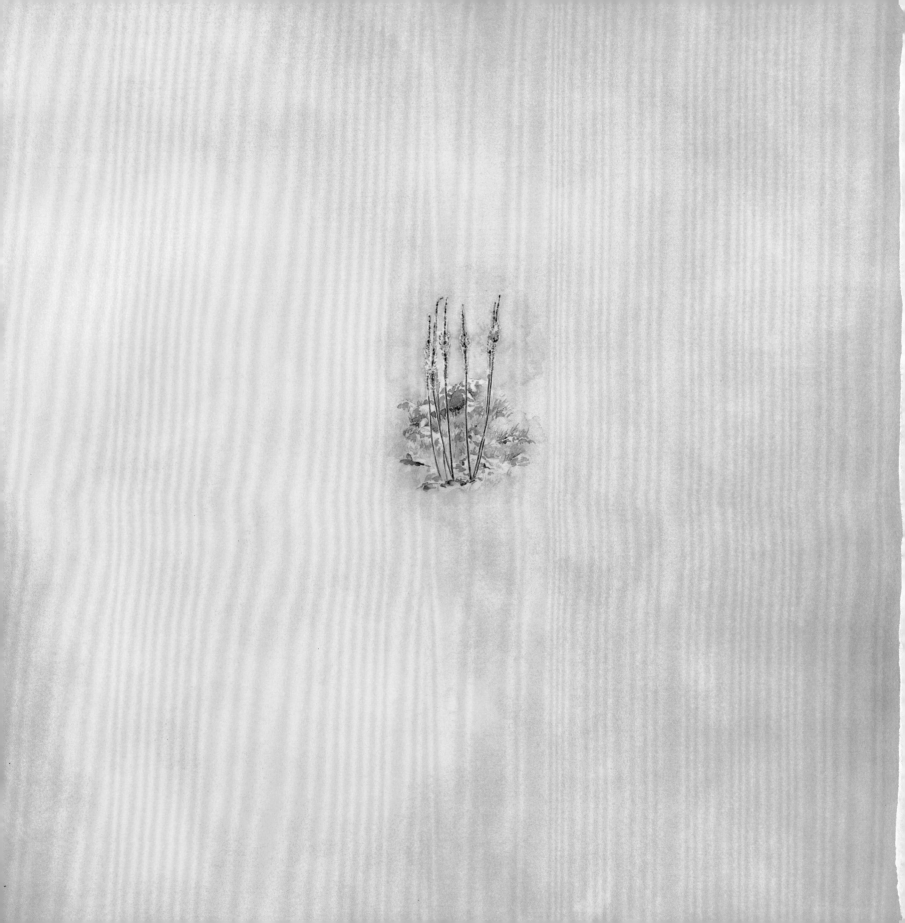